ZERO UNEMPLOYMENT IN KENYA

The Utility of Tajiriba Spaces

BY

GEOFFREYSON KHAMALA

i

Published By:

FOUNDATION
"Thinking for the Universe"

ISBN-13: 978-1508684640

ISBN-10: 1508684642

DEDICATION

I dedicate this book to thinking gurus, their admirers and critics worldwide.

TABLE OF CONTENTS

LIST OF ACRONYMS & ABBREVIATIONS

AKDN	-	Aga Khan Development Network
BCE	–	Before Common Era
CBK	-	Central Bank of Kenya
CE	-	Common Era
CORD	-	Coalition for Reforms and Democracy
COTU	-	Central Organization of Trade Unions
DNA	–	Deoxyribonucleic Acid
e.g.	-	For example
ERSWEC	-	Economic Recovery Strategy for Wealth and Employment Creation
etc.	-	et cetera
FKE	-	Federation of Kenya Employers
FPE	-	Free Primary Education
GDP	-	Gross Domestic Product
GEMA	-	Gikuyu, Embu, Meru and Akamba Association
GoK	-	Government of Kenya
i.e.	-	that is
ILO	-	International Labour Organization
KADU	-	Kenya African Democratic Union

KAMATUSA	-	Kalenjin, Maasai, Turkana and Samburu Association
KANU	-	Kenya African National Union
KNBS	-	Kenya National Bureau of Statistics
KPU	-	Kenya People's Union
LAPSSET	-	Lamu Port South Sudan Ethiopia Transport Corridor
LUTESA	-	Luhya, Teso and Sabaot Association
NARC	-	National Rainbow Coalition
NESC	-	National Social and Economic Council
NFD	-	Northern Frontier District
NSSF	-	National Social Security Fund
ODM	-	Orange Democratic Movement
PNU	-	Party of National Unity
SAPs	-	Structural Adjustment Programmes
UFAA	-	Unclaimed Financial Assets Authority
UN	-	United Nations
UN HABITAT	-	United Nations Human Settlement Programme
UNDP	-	United Nations Development Programme
US	-	United States

PUBLICATIONS BY GEOFFREYSON KHAMALA

1. The Perfect Theory: A Complete Unified Description of the Universe (2014)

2. What is science? Science as an Adaptive Capacity (2014)

3. Is Science Religion? (2014)

4. Wither Globalization Enter Connectedness (2014)

5. The Ultimate Theory: The Perfect Description of the Universe (2015)

6. Tajiriba Spaces: The Solution to Sub-Optimal Outcomes (2015)

7. Zero Unemployment in Kenya: The Utility of Tajiriba Spaces (2015)

8. Reclaiming the Sahara: A Case for Universal Connectedness (2015)

ABSTRACT

Practically half of Kenyans, about 21.5 million people, are poor. Ensuring citizens have an income is the single most effective means of transforming lives and reducing deep-rooted poverty and inequality. Regrettably, lack of income opportunities has become such a huge challenge in Kenya.

Many Kenyans leave school hoping to find work or start a viable business to participate in economic building, but for the last three decades income opportunities have not been forthcoming.

Statistics on joblessness and inactivity indicate that over 40 per cent Kenyans are without stable incomes. The joblessness and idleness crisis in Kenya, however, is just a symptom of something worse - relatedness.

Relatedness is the most significant constraint on the capacity of the Kenyan economy to grow and to create enough opportunities to accommodate the ever-increasing number of school-leavers (and school drop-outs).

Just about 10 million Kenyans of the working age are not gainfully engaged. The country needs to deliver at least 1,000,000 job opportunities every year for several years to serve the increasing number of jobless college graduates. Despite this, Kenya only manages to produce insignificant (116,000) new income opportunities annually.

In the face of the skyrocketing public wage bill, it is clear that employment expansion in the public sector is not a realistic alternative. Impliedly therefore, Kenya's struggle with unemployment can only be meaningfully resolved through the expansion of the private sector.

Whereas the public sector was devolved with the promulgation of the 2010 constitution, the private sector is yet to decentralize. As such, remote rural locations and urban slums possess unexploited potential.

Tajiriba Spaces are platforms of change, mechanisms for employment creation, opportunities for revenue creation and avenues for academic engagement and dialogue on policy matters in remote rural environments and informal settlements in urban centers.

Remote rural locations and urban slums are the next growth frontier. The strategy is to steadily transform neglected and disadvantaged geographical locations into future megacities.

By urbanizing neighborhoods through Tajiriba Spaces, it is possible to spur the Kenyan economy to create millions of new income opportunities, and to achieve zero unemployment.

Keywords: Tajiriba spaces, connectedness, relatedness, zero unemployment, urbanized neighborhoods

CHAPTER ONE

HOW RELATEDNESS CONTRIBUTES TO NEEDLESS POWER STRUGGLES AND UNEMPLOYMENT IN KENYA

INTRODUCTION

Statistics on inactivity, unemployment and underemployment represent key indicators of the effectiveness of economic growth in improving the welfare of ordinary citizens.

Government data indicates that Kenya's economy was by end of 2013 valued at Sh3.87 trillion up from Sh3.4 trillion a year earlier (KNBS, 2014). The country was from September 2014 classified as a lower middle-income status economy, sixteen (16) years ahead of the Vision 2030 schedule after the revision of the GDP from Sh3.87 trillion to Sh4.65 trillion.

Under Vision 2030, Kenya aims to become an upper middle class country (GoK, 2007). For a country to attain upper middle income status (statistical revision may not be enough) it needs to be at least 50 per cent urbanized. However, estimates indicate that by 2030 only one-third of Kenya's total population will be categorized as urban (United Nations, 2014).

The most significant challenge is how to turn Kenya's increasingly segmented urban expansion into inclusive growth. Pointedly, the statistics are grim. Just about half of Kenyans are poor despite the on paper expansion of the economy towards middle-income status. Wealth in the country is concentrated in the hands of a very small minority, and in major towns and cities.

To triple income per head to achieve and sustain 10 per cent GDP growth per annum requires a rethink of the existing urbanization practice. Hitherto urbanization has been via migration to major towns and cities. Most importantly, relatedness must be overcome.

ECONOMIC PERFORMANCE AND JOB PROSPECTS IN KENYA

Kenya is considered a lower middle income economy effective September 30, 2014 (World Bank, 2014). The country's aspiration to shade its low income economy status by 2030 seems to have materialized much earlier than anticipated after the rebasing of the GDP from Sh3.87 trillion to Sh4.65 trillion (World Bank, 2014).

Even then, available statistics paints a gloomy picture of Kenya's job and income market.

The public sector employee count stands at around 48.2% (700,000) while the private sector employs about 51.8 per cent of the Kenya's workforce. However, the public and private sector employee count combined constitutes not more than 10% of Kenya's total workforce.

Ninety (90) per cent of Kenya's total labor force earns a living from the informal (*jua kali*) sector (and small scale agriculture or subsistence farming and pastoralist activities). Evidently, for the last two decades hardly any formal jobs have been created. Most jobs in Kenya are created in smallholder agriculture and informal enterprises that do not yield much tax revenue to support public goods and services.

Despite being indispensable in creation of new income opportunities, the informal sector for the most part operates with little support from the public and private sectors of the economy.

Kenya's unemployment rate is over 40% (KNBS, 2014). By end of the year 2013, only 13.5 million out of an estimated 41.8 total population were gainfully engaged. Whereas about 800,000 Kenyans join the labour market annually, only about 150,000 (18.75%) of them become productively engaged.

More or less 10 million Kenyans of the working age are unemployed. Patently no person can enjoy dignified existence without a stable source of income. No wonder statistics show that nearly half of Kenyans (46%) live in abject poverty (World Bank, 2005; ISS, 2015).

RELATEDNESS THE BANE OF KENYA

Though many Kenyans are focused, innovative and hard-working, there are good reasons for the limited income opportunities in the formal sector.

Basically, job creation and enterprise development are in the province of individual and private enterprises. Besides, in terms of public and private infrastructure, a large urban-rural divide is quite evident. Sadly, without proper public and private infrastructure the private sector may be incapable or unenthusiastic to bear the infrastructural costs associated with

4

operating enterprises in uncertain and relatively less profitable markets.

However, the principal explanation as to why many Kenyan citizens have insufficient economic opportunity to apply their adaptive capacities is relatedness – the structuring of the Kenyan society into lineages, clans, ethnic groups, races, religions and civilizations.

Relatedness tends to polarize the public space through divisive politics, stifles economic activity, undermines progress, and therefore, affects the quality of life. Because of relatedness, the Kenyan economy has grown below its potential over the last several decades.

Relatedness is responsible for the lack of enough income opportunities and a weak job market.

Domestically, vested interests hinder growth and distributional goals and contribute to slower growth, fewer jobs, rural-urban migration, poverty and inequality, escalating crime rates, ethnic mobilization, internal conflicts, and terrorism.

Taking a more global strategic perspective, the problem is not the market economy per se but the neoliberal ideology, the thought process that informs globalization. The neoliberal dogma (globalization) derives from notions of limited resources, income opportunities and possibilities. However, according to connectedness Kenya is in possession of abundant resources, endless opportunities and infinite possibilities.

Over the past five decades, Kenya's politics and policy discourse has gyrated around identities. During this period, relatedness has made it extremely hard for the Kenyan economy to grow and create enough income opportunities. Ethnic polarization and discrimination is still pervasive in all spheres and sectors in the country.

The 2014 Economic Survey noted that Kenya's economy performed dismally in 2013 growing by only 4.7 per cent way below the Jubilee administration's target of 10 per cent and just one point improvement from 4.6 per cent growth recorded in 2012 (KNBS, 2014). The World Bank had projected a growth rate of 5 per cent.

According to the Kenya Government, the national economy missed its growth targets of 5.5 per cent weighed down by a host of issues ranging from uncertainty over the 2013 general election, rising incidents of insecurity and terrorism that impacted negatively on tourist arrivals, high government borrowing, and a high wage bill.

The other reasons include erratic weather that reduced agricultural production, high interest rates that limited borrowing by private sector and reduction in public expenditure during the transition year.

The official position does not belabor on tribal coalescing, mega-corruption, sectarian tensions and violence, skewed public appointments and impunity that are a threat to national unity.

On income opportunities, government statistics demonstrate that the government missed the target of a million jobs per year jobs to reduce the high rate of unemployment (KNBS, 2014). The economy generated 742,000 new jobs, 84 per cent (626,000) in the informal sector and 16 per cent (116,000) in the formal sector.

Observably, majority of the new jobs were created by the informal sector as a result of growth in the labour intensive segment. Out of the measly 116,000 new jobs in the formal sector, 26,300 jobs were in the public sector mainly on account of the implementation of devolved structures and employment of more teachers.

Devolution of the public sector, the centerpiece of the 2010 Constitution, has added to the size and cost of government exponentially. Subsequently, the productivity of Kenya's public sector and the accompanying wage bill has come under intense scrutiny. Critics consider the ballooning wage bill a drain on public resources that would otherwise be spent on development projects.

The public service has up to 700,000 employees and a wage bill of Ksh461 billion in 2012/2013.

In early 2014, the Kenya Government hinted that an estimated 100,000 civil servants could be rendered redundant in the 2014-2015 financial year in an attempt to contain the spiraling wage bill which stands at Sh458 billion per annum.

Historically, attempts by countries to reduce the number of civil servants by rendering some unemployed to reduce the wage bill by right-sizing, restructuring, downsizing, retrenching and streamlining or through tax hikes often hurt growth, breed new cycles of crippling unemployment and condemn millions of people to utter poverty.

For example, in 1994, the World Bank and the International Monetary Fund came up with the Structural Adjustment

Programmes (SAPs) that saw massive retrenchments from the public sector.

However, an unproductive, bloated, corrupt and vindictive public sector also hurts growth and job creation.

The annoyance in Kenya is relatedness.

Relatedness is essentially a form of public sector corruption. Relatedness frequently denies Kenyans income and job opportunities when resources are diverted to unproductive sectors.

Relatedness also reduces productivity and works as a disincentive to those who are innovative, creative and industrious. More importantly, rural and remote locations remain under-developed due to deliberate governmental policy informed by relatedness.

People join the public sector so that their relatives, cronies and friends could extract value from the public. This zero-sum brand of politics frequently polarizes the Kenyan society along faultlines as a predatory political class with the power to reward itself, cronies and communities jockey for positions on the national high table. The competition for the apparently limited jobs and tenders has inadvertently exacerbated the "us" and "them" feelings building up ethnic tensions, rivalry and even conflicts.

Oddly enough, the "us vs. them" mentality seems unlikely to abate much as long as the unemployment rate remains high and remote rural areas which are further away from major towns and cities continue being neglected.

Obviously, the most promising mechanism for defusing identity struggles is to ensure there are enough income opportunities for everyone.

Relatedness is responsible for the rise of extremist groups and separatist movements that challenge the legitimacy of state actors in the domestic and international ecosystem.

Indeed experience shows that when large parts of a country are neglected they may possibly be tempted to secede. Kenya secessionist stir (1963-1967) dubbed *shifta* war when ethnic Somalis in the Northern Frontier District (NFD) attempted to merge with their compatriots in Somalia.

Secessionist agitations have also been witnessed in Nigeria. During the Biafran secessionism probably two million people perished over the question of Nigerian unity. But it appears politicians never learn their lesson because today Nigeria's vast northeastern desert region remains beyond the control of the government out of neglect and it would take decades to correct this appalling mistake. Boko Haram (meaning Western education is harmful and forbidden) aware of the state of the impoverished north is involved in a bloody campaign to create an Islamic state. This has resulted in tremendous political instability in the worst affected northern states such as Borno, Adamawa, Kaduna, Bauchi, Yobe and Kano. Boko Haram's uprising has become a regional crisis jeopardizing peace and security in Nigeria, Cameroon, Chad and Niger.

Recently, millions of people lost their lives and/or were forcibly evicted from their homes in Egypt, Libya, Mali, Central African Republic and South Sudan, among others because of relatedness.

Relatedness comes in many shapes and forms. One of the most prominent strands is the demand for fair distribution of resources and correction of supposed historical marginalization. The other equally prominent strand is that in support of the status quo by those wanting to sustain privilege based on tyranny of numbers. Finally, another champions the formation of regional parties. Since independence, Kenya's political arena has tribal coalescing in the form of the Gikuyu, Embu, Meru and Akamba (Gema) association, the Kalenjin,

Maasai, Turkana and Samburu (*Kamatusa* and recently the Luhya, Teso and Sabaot (*Lutesa*) association.

On a possibly more positive light, Kenya has witnessed the formation of the Commonwealth of Coast Counties (*Jumuiya ya Kaunti za Pwani*), an economic bloc that seeks to bring together Mombasa, Kilifi, Kwale, Lamu, Tana River River and Taita-Taveta counties. Perceptibly, this is a welcome move to deal with historical neglect. However, it is also possible that these are simplistic and unhelpful narratives that create room for selfish leadership to thrive through divide-and-rule tactics.

There must be an alternative way to redress historical and current injustices based on a common value system and or geography (connectedness) rather than communities (relatedness).

Relatedness is a system of social hierarchy that provides short term stability and benefits where voters trade political support for emotional satisfaction.

Ideally, political parties are supposed to compete based on alternative policy prescriptions to exhilarate economic growth thereby creating more opportunities and jobs. Inauspiciously, over the past five decades, Kenya's politics has gyrated around identity politics. Villages and neighborhoods have been turned into ethnic enclaves.

When people are manipulated to build walls of partition, prejudice and hate, politicians become lazy, incompetent and tend to use divide-and-rule tactics to win power and latitude. These way politicians have an easy ride to power. Political parties are turned into mere vehicles for aspiring candidates with which to seek political office.

Besides, identity-based politics is adversarial, produces winners and losers and, as such, strains relationships.

Public sector corruption thrives where a country's discourse orbits around relatedness making the state incapable of managing inequalities, animosity and possible conflicts between supposedly different groups during election time when people need to be rendered unable to vote freely, or at all. This was apparent in Kenya in 1992, 1997 and 2007.

Many Kenyans attribute the Kenyan problem as having originated with colonialism among other extraneous causes and fail to acknowledge that Kenyans are partly responsible for their own undoing. Slavery, colonialism, neo-colonialism, patrimonialism, neo-patrimonialism and other forms of imperialism are actually manifestations of relatedness.

Today we live and experience relatedness (internal challenges) in the form of struggles based on ethnic affiliations among other identity formations.

Colonialism is in the past. Therefore, identity struggles and conflicts in independent Kenya must trigger self-examination, quiet reflection and the impulse to revisit the relatedness question with sobriety.

Relatedness is an adaptive capacity. Long before recorded history, relatedness originated as mechanisms to sustain life. The incest taboo, which is almost universal and that has a biological basis, besides preventing the health setbacks associated with inbreeding, it also helps to avoid competition and conflict that may lead to premature death within the family household.

The survival of the family and existing societal organization and patterns rests on the control of sex among its members and the consequent need for other family units as sources of spouses. The incest taboo normally extends to close (and sometimes distant) relatives for the same purpose thus bringing into its fold lineages and exogamic clans.

The family and the successive socio-political identities are therefore adaptive capacities to extend life and sidestep bereavement. Unluckily, human socio-political and economic institutions simply solidify human groups, deflect and externalize competition, conflict and death.

In the early days, relatedness was inevitable because human societies spent years isolated from each other as they lacked a common language and were separated by geographical features such as deserts, forests, rivers, lakes, oceans and mountains. During the early days human beings were also susceptible to both vagaries of nature, human-induced disasters and general insecurity.

The present state system, international law and international norms have made the world more connected, less violent and more attuned to the endurance of life. We are even headed toward a world in which everyone will speak the same language. Therefore, relatedness as a mechanism of protecting life has gradually been replaced by more viable mechanisms.

Relatedness depends on paternity during pregnancy. Maternal parentage is largely ignored. However, the random nature of the circumstances of the human birth process makes it fairly impossible to accurately predict and verify one's community of birth. Even if it were possible such information is unhelpful in a connectedness environment.

An old joke is told of a son who sought blessings from his father to marry. But every time the son identified a girl he thought was ideal the father would intimate the girl was actually the boy's sister. This went for some time until after the sixth attempt the boy in frustration sought his mother's advice. The mother confided in the son to marry any of the six girls he had earlier identified because the supposed male parent was not actually the biological father to the boy.

This anecdote may seem to confirm the often repeated phrase that only the woman knows the actual father to her child. Even then, evidence abounds showing even women cannot conclusively establish maternal relationship. Parental testing (paternity test, maternity test or both) is required to establish fully genetic proof on whether two individuals have a biological parent–child relationship. Every person inherits half of their DNA from their biological mother and the other half from their biological father.

The downside is that assuming paternal biological relationship as in relatedness has largely had negative effects since individuals and groups have used such assumptions to attempt disastrously to project power, prestige and wealth locally, regionally or even throughout the world.

History is the record of our past symbols (especially language), myths (origin and migration myths) and rituals (birth rituals, naming rituals which dictate our last names or surnames, puberty rituals (coming of age), marriage rituals and death rituals (mourning). Sadly, because of relatedness our past associations and struggles have been painful and bloody. This is because every community has symbols, myths and rituals boasting of its own consequence relative to others.

According to connectedness, history records our past engagements and efforts in the quest to stay alive. Mourning is a life-affirming ritual. Knowledge of our historical roots is only important if it adds value to our life experiences. However, if such knowledge only adds pain, mistrust and suspicion then it is not considered necessary.

Historically all Kenyans are recent migrants into Kenya. While Kenya is reputed to be the site of human origin, the inhabitants of current Kenya relocated from elsewhere (i.e. parts of the African continent, Middle East, Europe and Asia).

The persistence of relatedness is proving to be disruptive to Kenya's productivity, stability and development. Today, the biggest misleading notion is that Kenya is a multi-ethnic state primarily inhabited by Bantu, Nilotic and Cushitic populations. Manifestly, relatedness is responsible for the large social inequalities in Kenya.

Relatedness and connectedness are two sides of the same coin in the quest to understand and tame the world. For the most part of human history, the human society has been demarked along different faultiness namely familial networks (relatedness), class (the haves vis-à-vis have-nots), parties (minority vis-à-vis majority) and linguistic diversity (minority languages vis-à-vis majority languages).

People often feel they are in charge of their fate and destiny when they coalesce as groups. However, relatedness exposes humanity to untold carnage, orgies of criminal mayhem, and ghastly and indiscriminate slaughter and trauma.

The alternative path is connectedness. Connectedness is candid about unity but deliberately hushed on diversity. Kenyans are one regardless of the supposed diversity. According to connectedness, Kenya is one people united by their quest for life. The Kenyan state represents the evolution of human society in the quest to protect life.

Connectedness frees humanity from being bogged down by sideshows that include competition, discrimination, stereotyping, etc. so as to best confront the boundary between life and death.

Contemporary Kenyan societies have long ceased to depend on nature for existence. They use technology to manipulate their environment to sustain life. Kenyans have since acquired mutually intelligible languages. The two official languages in Kenya are English and Swahili. The world is witnessing the end of an epoch and the start of a milestone. Relatedness seems to have run out of steam since it is no longer sustainable. However, the Kenyan people are yet to rise above relatedness.

Kenya's situation calls for policy innovation and non-conventional policy thinking to overcome relatedness. Relatedness mostly benefits sly, selfish and sycophantic politicians lacking viable policy positions to take Kenya from Point A to Point B. Devious politicians use relatedness to perpetually exploit the vulnerability of their hoodwinked electorates to remain in power without offering alternative policy prescription to facilitate societal progress.

To prevent Kenyans from being divided along linguistic, religious, racial, gender, regional, tribal and/or ethnic lines, leadership must orbit around the aptitude to mobilize people behind sustainable agendas.

Kenya's Vision 2030 is anchored on three key pillars namely economic, social and political governance (GoK, 2007). On the economic front, a sustained growth rate of 10% is envisioned. The social pillar envisages a fair and united society characterized by unbiased collective progress. On the political front, the vision vouches for a viable party system as a way to institutionalize free and fair elections and to guarantee legitimate governance.

With pro-active engagement between informed citizens and enlightened leadership it is possible to usher in connectedness. Connectedness is guided by the values of purpose-driven free enterprise, inclusivity and shared prosperity. Average Kenyans prefer an open democratic polity with guarantees that public power and resources are deployed for public benefit.

Through the lens of connectedness it is possible to achieve a cohesive and united Kenyan society. It is also possible to institute a credible political system that is anchored on policy positions and alternatives.

WHAT MUST BE DONE TO FIX RELATEDNESS

Achieving zero unemployment, such that each person can utilize productively their adaptive capacity, is an ideal which every country hopes to accomplish. Yet it is near impossible to achieve perfect employment in an environment polluted by relatedness. Kenya's economy remains largely informal because of relatedness. Kenya is not an exception. Many countries in the world are also still grappling with the question of relatedness.

For the case of Kenya, this study vouches for the introduction of Tajiriba Spaces. Tajiriba Spaces are urban settings in rural and remote areas. Through Tajiriba Spaces, it is possible to guarantee adequate income opportunities for everyone in Kenya.

The design and implementation of urbanized neighborhoods in rural (and remote) areas can boost Kenya's political, economic and social systems, grow Kenya's economy and scale up income opportunities guided by a six-point plan namely to:

i. Stimulate the rise of the periphery
   a) Give voice to a cadre of Kenyans who don't identify with relatedness.

b) Encourage enterprise in remote geographical locations and low income areas including urban slums to deal with historical and contemporary neglect.

c) Promote inclusivity and shared prosperity.

a) Capitalize on neighborhood linkages and diplomacy to promote trade, cooperation and peaceful relations.

ii. Devolve the private sector

a) Initiate infrastructural development to attract private sector investments in remote rural locations and urban slums.

b) Support enterprise - neighborhood enterprises and neighborhood tourism and conferencing.

iii. Devolve dialogue

a) Make neighborhoods the focus of policy

b) Decentralize scholarly dialogue

c) Provoke issue-based politics at the grassroots

iv. Change the neighborhood

b) Turn neighborhoods from ethnic enclaves into points of interaction, trade, exchange and communication.

c) Urbanize hamlets and villages.

d) Reward excellence, achievement, merit, enterprise, innovation and talent right from the neighborhood level.

e) Empower neighborhoods to pro-actively participate in policy initiation, design, implementation, monitoring and evaluation.

f) Facilitate neighborhood linkages and neighborhood diplomacy to promote peaceful contacts and exchange.

v. Reshape politics

a) Encourage politics to resonate with shared values and/or alternative policy perspectives.

b) Discourage identity politics which revolves around communities.

c) Proactively engage politicians and their spouses in between elections.

d) Center the experience of average Kenyans which is about security, food security, the environment, infrastructure, education, health, sanitation etc. instead of supremacy discourse and marginalization that resonates with competition for power, resources and mating partners among political, intellectual and economic elites.

e) Make politics value-driven - Allow politics to resonate with the principal law of the universe which is collective life preservation.

vi. Proclaim life-preservation as an overriding principle

a) Deter and punish all forms of violence.

b) Protect the environment.

c) Outlaw capital punishment.

CONCLUSION

Kenya has adequate human and material resources. Unfortunately, these resources are frequently misallocated, misapplied, underutilized and/or unused because of relatedness. According to connectedness, politics can be value-driven. With purpose-driven (political) leadership and a dynamic citizenry committed to instituting an open democratic polity, inclusive economic growth and the right fiscal and monetary policy mix, zero unemployment is achievable.

Connectedness is where the public sector, the private sector and the nonprofit sector work together to create value. While relatedness restricts the flow of resources, connectedness unleashes endless possibilities.

CHAPTER TWO

THE RISE OF THE PERIPHERY IN KENYA

INTRODUCTION

The biggest quandary in Kenya is relatedness. Kenya has excellent weather conditions and well trained, productive and self-driven citizens but the country suffers inequalities in development, communal conflicts are common and entrenched poverty is prevalent all because of relatedness.

Relatedness is commonly typified by unequal relations and strategic mistrust between groups of political actors deemed to represent Kenya's supposed 42 disparate communities.

Political, intellectual and economic elites in Kenya use identities as a tool for self-seeking political, scholarly and economic agendas.

The Kenyan dilemma is how to usefully commit the huge human capital and material resources available in the country. Identity politics and struggles have guaranteed the misuse and/or underutilization of the vast natural resources and the huge human capital available in the country. Forced idleness swallow up growth and ties down future generations.

Many Kenyans have not benefited from the country's economic growth because the current growth model consigns a huge chunk of people living in remote undeveloped regions of the country to poverty and neglect. Those in urban slums fair no better. This has largely been due to the lack of policy, legislation and/or implementable interventions on taming relatedness.

Kenya must invest in all of her people and open up business and investment opportunities in the country's remote rural areas and urban slums to correct sub-par outcomes. Tajiriba Spaces are attempts to commence and support profitable investment in remote rural locations to help provide better material life for all Kenyans and lessen to zero the number of jobless Kenyans.

GIVING VOICE TO THE AVERAGE KENYAN CITIZEN

Average Kenyans are pawns in a sophisticated power-play between predatory cliques of political, intellectual and economic actors.

As things stand today, the ordinary Kenyan citizen does not aspire to hold public office. However, average citizens in

Kenya expect the government to deliver basics at the least. They want politics to be about them not about the self-interested politician. They expect politicians to package themselves with attractive offers and/or policy prescriptions on how if given leadership opportunities they will be able to deliver goods and services to move society from point A to point B.

Sadly, politicians prefer shortcuts. They exploit cleavages to rally support. Once in power, they use racial, ethnic, regional and/or religious characteristics as a basis for making governmental decisions. Little wonder decades after independence, state building and balanced development remain a pipedream.

Relatedness is the reason why government policies rarely align with the preferences and genuine interests of average Kenyan citizens.

Oddly enough, non-investment in geographical gray areas informed by relatedness normally leads to perceptions of marginalization and ultimately self-destruction when the disparity becomes overly pronounced.

Relatedness tempts people to spent lots of energy on brutal contests and issues that do not add value. From time to time,

Kenyans find themselves locked in supremacy wars as they compete for recognition and space. This jostling frequently raises ethnic tension and causes frequent hostilities between communities.

Certainly, remote rural environments fail to attract investments partly due to the fear of political tensions every election year. Why do we allow such situations?

The most effective way to is to institute a mental shift from a zero-sum mentality to avoid needless power struggles. On this score, embracing connectedness may help collapse boundaries along fault lines. Through Tajiriba Spaces, it should be possible to empower voters/citizens to be able to select leaders who would not abuse their collective trust.

Today, the Kenyan society is much more open-minded and cosmopolitan such that the average citizen, if given voice, might not be ready to repeat the shameful passivity and eagerness to pay attention to diversionary conversations that has made the country witness competition, suspicion and bloodletting along fault lines. People don't want to carry with them dastardly crimes committed by other people or that they were made to commit.

Going forward, many Kenyans may prefer to identify with the margins as they endeavor to touch the lives of ordinary people in their neighborhoods and far-flung areas in a bid to end polarization.

Whilst in the past people were categorized as either male of female today there are more than two distinctions after the emergence of a third gender (gender queer, intersex and transgender). Today, there are many people who are legally recognized in parts of the world as being neither male nor female.

Similarly, more and more Kenyans are starting to consider themselves as non-categorized or identityless except in terms of shared values and or geography. For such people, segmentation on the basis of familial, kinship, ethnic obligations or other affinities is past its sale date.

THE VALUE OF INCLUSIVITY AND SHARED PROSPERITY

Relatedness makes some people feel superior and others to feel marginalized undermining efforts to build trust and have wealth broadly shared.

The non-categorized don't feel like being part of such mind-games. They don't belong to the right, the left or the center. They are contended with being on the periphery and prefer inclusivity since they believe in shared prosperity.

Those on the periphery see politics in broader terms. Politics is more than simply a public activity that looks after the collective interests of specific identities, and political parties are not mere vehicles for aspiring candidates with which to seek election. Political parties and interest groups must be guided by the overriding resolve to sustain life.

To appeal to those on the periphery, political parties have no choice but to repackage their policy prescriptions so that they don't mix politics and relatedness.

Those on the periphery appreciate that development is inseparable from universal values. The expectation is that detribalized non-sectarian parties and that are truly inclusive in terms of hierarchies, structures and membership will pursue inclusivity through policy prescriptions that mirror the will of the universe rather than to mirror the will of the electors.

Breaking the barriers erected by relatedness is not easy but someday the periphery (connectedness) will become the dominant thought process. In the near term, to be elected to a public office one will have to transcend relatedness. So, relatedness may be today's mainstream but change is occurring at the margins.

Through Tajiriba Spaces it should be possible to create millions of new work opportunities in the country enabling many millions of Kenyans to be financially secure.

URBANIZE REMOTE RURAL LANDSCAPES

More than half of the world's population (approximately 54%) now lives in urban areas (UN, 2014). Sustainable urbanization is a desired outcome worldwide. The time-honored expectation is that urbanization makes society less insular. Urban locations host people from different parts of Kenya and the world. The expectation is that many people will come from far and wide to inhabit Tajiriba Spaces. They will consider these urbanized neighborhoods their home[1].

Kenya is the way it is (i.e. rural-urban divide) because of zoning. During the times of colonialism and immediately after, zoning was viable. Parts of the country were designated

---

[1] According to Khamala (2005b) home is where you realize the meaning of your life and perhaps assist others to ascertain the purpose and meaning of their existence.

into cities, forests, catchment areas, industrial zones, urban zones and even agricultural zones. However, many decades later on there is increased demand for mixed developments. Today, it is possible to find many areas with residential housing, expansive shopping malls, as well as offices.

Most rural locations in Kenya are intolerably underdeveloped partly because of zoning. Whereas agriculture is the mainstay of the rural economy, over-population, small land sizes, inefficient farming techniques, and poor post-harvest handling and storage facilities make the productivity and growth of the agricultural sector problematic. This is partly why for long villages have been associated with economies of affection (Hyden, 1980) and politics of the belly (Bayart, 1993).

Kenya has a long way to end poverty and inequality since economic growth is restricted to urban areas for the reason that the focus of the economy is on the urban elite.

Inequalities informed by the rural-urban divide are often a function of location, policy choices and leadership. The most challenging aspect is how heal the social inequalities and the tension that accompanies relatedness as a result of real or imagined competition.

Kenya is mostly rural although urbanization is the rise. It is important to increase the pace of urbanization neglected corners of Kenya to grow Kenya's economy. It is necessary to transform remote rural neighborhoods into sizeable urban clusters to facilitate economic betterment. Tajiriba Spaces are proactive interventions to address historical and current injustices premised on geography rather than communities.

Through Tajiriba Spaces, it is possible to empower ordinary Kenyans to invest in their neighborhoods to increase the rate of urbanization such that rural dwellers can access urban services and jobs while sustainably utilizing available and potential arable land.

The crucial component of this strategy is for neighborhoods to focus on domestic consumption (address weak consumer demand through creation of new income opportunities) and to trade surpluses beyond their borders to grow their revenues.

NEIGBORHOOD SECURITY

Every Kenyan wants to live in a safe neighborhood. Lack of income opportunities coupled with a deep-set sense of perpetual suspicion and mistrust among Kenyans makes neighborhoods unsafe. Those not gainfully engaged must somehow find something to do to earn a living. Some people may engage in crime because they are idle and unemployed. This is because unemployment breeds sideshows such as misery, deprivation and despair.

Neighborhood security closely correlates with the availability of adequate income opportunities. It is only after we have dealt with the lack of adequate income opportunities that we can effectively guarantee neighborhood security. So, building Tajiriba Spaces can have added positive effect of reducing crime and general insecurity.

NEIGBORHOOD DIPLOMACY

There are a category of people who perceive and engage the world from the understanding that it is borderless, seamless and boundless. In this category lie the thinker, the visionary, the inventor, the innovator, the entrepreneur and the peacemaker. For this category of people, relatedness is limiting, shortsighted and a distraction.

The state system was designed to fail for the majority of the population for encouraging a zero-sum brand of politics informed by relatedness. Relatedness dictates that governments spent more and more resources on state arms and armaments. Military spending on warplanes, missile systems, surveillance equipment, warships and armored cars poses a security dilemma since other countries feel threatened and resort to spending to counter the perceived threat. On the whole, military spending diminish resources and productive income opportunities.

Tajiriba Spaces presents the opportunity to engineer grassroots diplomacy with the neighborhood as the point of reference hoping to render world militaries to be of no use with the passage of time.

A borderless Kenya is the better alternative path to ensuring adequacy of income opportunities. Instead of building walls of separation and discrimination, the focus is on being better neighbors.

PURPOSE-DRIVEN UNIQUE DIGITAL IDENTIFIER

Scientists discern the offerings of nature for human comfort, convenience and advantage. Because of relatedness, people's identity is primarily premised on paternity, inheritance of surnames, and a combination of both, among other features of identifications that are based on fault lines.

Today, science has made tremendous strides such that it possible to capture each person's bio-data for purposes of unique identification. It should be possible to establish a universal identification system consisting of biometric information (biological markers such as facial image, finger prints and iris scan) that can uniquely make out every traceable person.

In a connectedness world, humanity can embrace a more scientific way for tracing the peopling of the world. The use of unique biological identifiers can render the current identification that is premised on core human identities like person's race, religion, ethnicity and/or gender pointless.

Through Tajiriba Spaces, it should be possible to promote the mapping of the human genome as part of the process of achieving connectedness.

ENTERPRISE AT THE MARGINS OF CONNECTEDNESS

Enterprise is the key driver of economic growth as well as the creation of income opportunities. Majority of the jobs in Kenya are in the private sector. Even then, most of these jobs are of poor quality. This is because the informal economy contributes 90 per cent to the job market in the country. Through the establishment of Tajiriba Spaces it is possible to tap the huge human capital available in the country but that is currently outside the armpits of the formal economy. Remote rural locations and urban slums can have the chance to exploit the currently huge but untapped market potential.

Expedient way of shopping is trending the world over. Tajiriba Spaces can provide one-stop access to a complete range of goods, services and opportunities under one roof. Tajiriba Spaces can be home to local, continental and global retail and wholesale brands. People in marginal areas can be able to conveniently reside, dine, shop, bank and relax, all under the same roof.

When complete, each Tajiriba Space can comprise among other facilities expansive retail malls, shopping centres, commercial premises, office blocks, hotels, eateries, slaughter houses, banking halls, hospitals, manicured homes, day care centers, professional facilities, industrial parks, entertainment outlets and arenas for staging shows and concerts in Kenya's remote rural environments.

Hitherto wealth has been concentrated in privileged urban areas and cities contributing to extreme inequality, poverty, rural-urban migration, urban crime, urban gridlock, overcrowding, poor sanitation and unhealthy living conditions.

Tajiriba Spaces can encourage spatial agglomeration and act as a catalyst for wider economic benefits. For example, Tajiriba Spaces in remote rural locations can help manage the housing deficit being experienced in major towns and cities which often lead to the mushrooming of urban slums. Still, because birthrates tend to fall along with economic development, through Tajiriba Spaces it is possible to manage population growth.

Nowadays individuals are taking much longer than earlier generations to finish schooling and settle into a career. Even then, a college diploma does not guarantee an internship, job or career. Through Tajiriba Spaces, it is possible to absorb interns in and out college under the internship programme.

By and large, students can be kept busy as they try to enter the workforce in a still-uncertain job market. Through the internships students can gain valuable experience that can prepare them for industry and life after university. Finally, an internship is also an opportunity to learn to volunteer, which is critical to connectedness.

CONCLUSION

Contests for political positions, prestige and wealth along fault lines by political, economic and intellectual actors so that they can manipulate resource allocation and use often breeds suspicion, stereotypes, misgivings and conflicts among Kenyans. This spells doom for job creation interventions and the development of marginal areas.

Kenya is typically rural with specific communities predominating different parts of the country. Political actors have subsequently zoned off parts of Kenya along imaginary communal boundaries thereby denying Kenyans the much-needed opportunity for reciprocal trust, inclusivity and shared prosperity.

It is vital to recognize and celebrate ordinary Kenyans whose frame of mind is attuned to connectedness to disengage the whole country from relatedness. This means urbanizing remote rural landscapes to facilitate reciprocated inflows and outflows of people from all parts of Kenya and the world into and out of rural and marginal areas.

Tajiriba Spaces are key channels for promoting urbanization, inclusivity, shared prosperity, neighborhood security, neighborhood diplomacy, social cohesion and trust and enterprise in remote rural geographical locations throughout the country.

CHAPTER THREE

DEVOLVE THE PRIVATE SECTOR

INTRODUCTION

Kenya's political and geographical reality radically changed when power and resources were devolved to the regions following the promulgation of the 2010 constitution.

Under the re-organization stipulated by the 2010 constitution, the country's eight provinces were replaced with 47 county administrations namely: Mombasa, Kwale, Kilifi, Tana River, Garissa, Wajir, Mandera, Marsabit, Isiolo, Meru, Tharaka-Nithi, Embu, Kitui, Machakos, Makueni, Nyandarua, Nyeri, Kirinyaga, Murang'a, Kiambu, Turkana, West Pokot, Samburu, Trans Nzoia, Uasin Gishu, Elgeyo-Marakwet, Nandi, Baringo, Laikipia, Nakuru, Narok, Kajiado, Kericho, Bomet, Kakamega, Vihiga, Bungoma, Busia, Siaya, Kisumu, Homa Bay, Migori, Kisii, Nyamira and Nairobi.

The devolution of political, fiscal and administrative components bestowed the powers of managing county affairs on elected leaders. The decentralized governance system was meant to tame the overconcentration of power and resources in the imperial presidency and the three big cities namely Nairobi, Mombasa and Kisumu.

Devolution is considered one of the best things that ever happened to Kenya's remote rural locations and urban slums. Now it is possible for public investments to be fairly distributed even in areas that initially lacked much in terms of basic infrastructure (transport, health, education, water, energy, and sanitation and sewer systems).

Nonetheless, there is a marked difference between the devolution of the public sector (political, fiscal and administrative units) and the private sector (individual and private enterprise). Kenya's private sector is concentrated in cities and major towns. To significantly decongest major towns and cities, jobs and opportunities must be created in remote rural locations and urban slums.

Devolution was meant to ensure equitable sharing of national and local resources throughout Kenya. The 47 counties were created to impel growth and development and address resource distribution grievances after decades of centralized maladministration. However, the devolution of the public sector alone is not enough. Neighborhoods need to be opened up for investment, urbanization and human traffic.

BENEFITS FOR DEVOLVING THE PRIVATE SECTOR

Kenya's public sector was devolved in 2010 but the private sector is yet to devolve to enable the whole country to enjoy fully the benefits of enterprise.

The private sector thrives best when there is effective economic demand (stable incomes). For the private sector to decentralize there is need for a market (people with disposable income) and the right mix of public and private infrastructure to support enterprise.

Many Kenyans expect their government to solve the unemployment problem. When put this way, a guaranteed basic monthly income to every Kenyan is the easiest way to address unemployment.

The benefits of a basic income on a national scale would be wide-ranging. First, the overall economy benefits if everyone has money to spend. Next, there are the obvious psychological benefits of knowing you can always afford food, clothing and shelter. Then there's the societal stability factor.

Unfortunately, nobody wants to be dependent on the public sector for freebies. This is because economic efficiency and personal freedom are tied with private property, free market institutions and enterprise.

Besides, when the wage bill takes a disproportionate share of a country's resources and is not accompanied by productivity, the sustainability of economy is threatened.

Finally, state-provided free goodies for social welfare could help the extremely poor people to cope with hardships but do not offer a lasting solution to poverty and inequality.

The public sector also has other drawbacks. Due to corruption, unchecked spending and misuse of government resources, there is a tendency for wealth to be concentrated in a few hands.

The cost of high, irregular, and wasteful public expenditures manifest as severe wage bill crisis, high interest rates, imposition of unsustainable levies and taxes, rampant insecurity and struggling economy.

Often, to cut down on runaway expenditure most governments introduce austerity measures. However, when all fails and when government recurrent expenditure consumes the bulk of the budget the economy stagnates or simply collapses.

A country's economy is said to have collapsed when there is too much money chasing too few goods (shortages) or when people queue for nothing in the street.

Much of government operations the world over are financed from taxes, fees fines and debts. Inopportunely, the Kenya Government is mostly a net consumer/importer not a net producer/exporter. The Kenya Government earns its revenue through various forms of levies and taxes.

Therefore, the hard reality is that most jobs will have to be created, not by the Kenya Government, but through individual and private enterprise. The Kenya Government is expected to provide a favorable climate for the private sector to thrive. Good governance, tax incentives and grants are needed to reduce the cost of doing business, grow the manufacturing sector, attract investments in industrial plants and encourage transformation of agriculture. Government stability and the provision of security are important to sustain tourism.

The private sector is the backbone of the Kenyan economy. Mega government capital intensive projects such as the Lamu Port South Sudan Ethiopia Transport Corridor (LAPSSET), standard gauge railway, laptops for Standard One pupils and one million-acre Galana irrigation scheme are oiled by the productivity of the private sector.

Trouble is that the private sector has not been growing fast enough to provide many sustainable jobs and revenue sources. Without a vibrant private sector, the government (and counties) would lose revenue that would have been generated from the sector and resort to monetization of its fiscal deficit. For example, the Kenya Government used the changed the changed wealth status after rebasing its economy in 2014 to increase the country's borrowing limit from Kshs. 1.2 trillion to Kshs. 2.5 trillion.

The general consensus, so far at least, is that the private sector is vital to a country's economy. The private sector compliments the state in the provision of goods and services. Therefore, a way must be found to unleash the muscle of the private sector if and when the public sector fails or is unwilling to do so through appropriate monetary and fiscal policies.

Hitherto the non-profit sector (civil society, interest groups, pressure groups, faith-based organizations, voluntary organizations, think-thanks, etc.) have basically restricted to affect government policy or government actions to benefit themselves or their cause. The non-profit sector can do more than merely bringing issues to the attention of the public, media and government, and/or providing humanitarian relief in times of emergencies.

Through Tajiriba Spaces, it is possible to facilitate the devolution of the private sector, stimulate neighborhood enterprises and neighborhood tourism and conferencing to transform the lives of ordinary Kenyans in the villages spread across the country.

Tajiriba Spaces are instruments addressing and redressing unequal and skewed development. Instead of intrigues, sideshows and maneuverings, the focus should be on production and infrastructural development in neglected zones to create income and job opportunities.

Each neighborhood can manage to generate thousands of jobs directly and indirectly. In the near term, Tajiriba Spaces have the potential to create inestimable investment opportunities and approximately 8,272,000 (2,068,000 direct and 6,204,000 indirect) jobs in Kenya inside 10 years. Therefore, it is possible to create slightly over 827,000 income opportunities in a year. This is based on the assumption that each Tajiriba Space can have the capacity to offer direct employment to approximately 4,000 people and thrice the number indirectly.

A typical neighborhood has several homesteads and close to 2,000 people. Some neighborhoods have a population of 2,000+. Therefore, jobless Kenyans can bank on Tajiriba Spaces in their locality or neighborhood for income opportunities.

The implication is that in the long term, Tajiriba Spaces have the potential of lifting hundreds of millions of people out of chronic and concentrated poverty and managing rural-urban migration.

ENTERPRISE IN REMOTE RURAL LOCATIONS

The private sector is a key partner in the growth and development of Kenya's economy.

Kenya's Vision 2030 development blueprint target of 10 per cent economic growth by 2050 was set to be achieved through the creation of special economic zones, namely, agricultural, industrial and technology parks (GoK, 2007). Besides, the Jubilee government pledged to build an enterprise economy by introducing tax breaks for the private sector.

Therefore, support and growth of the private sector is critical to the attainment of double-digit growth. This is because wealth creation occurs at the margins of public and private sectors with the nonprofit sector acting as the facilitator.

The nonprofit sector support projects that are economically sound but not financially viable in the short term. The sector acts as a subsidy to move such projects to the bankability stage. This way, the nonprofit sector fills the gap in development spending while the government gains from increased economic activity and revenue.

Through Tajiriba Spaces, it is possible to promote enterprise in marginal areas. The presence of Tajiriba Spaces could stem the exodus of talent from rural areas to major towns and cities. Tajiriba Spaces can act as one stop complex for all kinds of businesses and offices.

The diaspora is very important stakeholder and partner in development due to the kind of resources it has. Kenya's Central Bank figures show that Kenya's diaspora remits about $100 billion (US$1298310 million) (CBK, 2014). Through Tajiriba Spaces, it is possible to enhance the engagement with the diaspora to promote enterprise in remote geographical locations throughout the country.

NEIGHBORHOOD ENTERPRISES

For a long time, rural areas have been associated with low and erratic incomes. Most villagers remain by and large unemployed. No wonder many rural trading centers are dotted with abandoned infrastructural structures.

Nonetheless, local entrepreneurship must be scaled up for the Kenyan economy to take off. This is because start-ups are where most jobs are created.

The three sources of economic growth are labour force, investment and productivity. People in marginal areas have limited prospects because they have low access to credit, opportunities and markets. The gains to be made by overcoming these constraints are immense.

Through Tajiriba Spaces, it is possible to inspire an upsurge in demand for credit and neighborhood enterprises. Through neighborhood enterprises it is possible to utilize idle labour to boost productivity, income and employment opportunities.

Neighborhoods must strive to become magnets for entrepreneurs. Through neighborhood enterprises, village units can target to produce more goods and services for own consumption and satisfaction and to sell, exchange or donate any surpluses to other neighborhoods.

Governments benefit when people are able to work because a working populace means increased productivity and an expanded tax base.

More than 90 per cent of subsistence farmers cannot break even. Peasant farmers spend more resources to maintain their crop compared to what they eventually earn per acre. Tajiriba Spaces can help turn most subsistence farms into truly commercial undertakings by providing a ready market in close proximity.

Commercial/irrigated agriculture can co-exist with pockets of subsistence farming. Commercial agriculture can increase the amount of acreage that does not rely on rain-fed agriculture and also encourage the planting of high-value crops.

Tajiriba Spaces may also provide the necessary incentive to entrepreneurs to venture into processing and marketing of livestock products. This can be done by encouraging the setting up of modern abattoirs to provide market for livestock farmers and add value to animal products.

NEIGHBORHOOD TOURISM AND CONFERENCING

Starting and growing enterprise in remote rural environments has been made unnecessarily hard. This is basically because enterprise depends on the size and level of income (employment opportunities and business contracts). Evidently remote rural locations suffer from market failures.

Therefore, neighborhood tourism and conferencing can be used to attract and maintain a continuous flow of people with disposable income, in all the neighborhoods, to grow rural economies and generate jobs.

Upon completion, each Tajiriba Space will accommodate approximately 10,000 residents and 2,000 day visitors.

Successful neighborhoods will be those that are attractive to people looking for a better life. The implication is that neighborhood units will have to be turned into points of trade, interaction, exchange and communication.

Travel is a great provider of knowledge. Most rural dwellers rarely leave their village and as such know little of the larger world. However, this scenario is likely to change shortly as neighborhood tourism becomes the norm rather than the exception. Through Tajiriba Spaces, ordinary people and rural folks can get the opportunity to travel and explore the rest of the country and the world.

Through Tajiriba Spaces, ordinary Kenyans and rural folks can get the opportunity to sample Kenya's many tourist destinations; beautiful beaches; spectacular landscapes; stunning topography such as snow-capped mountains and deserts; impressive rock formations, hills and valleys; gorges; natural caves; water springs; seemingly endless grasslands; archaeological sites and museums; breathe taking view points; magnificent rivers; indigenous forests inhabited by rare birds and plants and other eye-catching wildlife; and other natural spaces.

Neighborhood tourism and conferencing can also help many people to overcome widely held beliefs about people, places and things (stereotypes).

Tajiriba Spaces can also prepare neighborhoods to allow and embrace continuous inflows and outflows of people wanting to share in their affluence. Flourishing new metropolis will be those teeming with new ideas, businesses, residents and anticipation. The expectation is that the arrival of new residents, tourists, resources and ideas in neighborhoods will result in dramatic change to benefit remote rural locations.

CONCLUSION

Kenyans chose to have a devolved system of government so that people can address their issues at local levels. There are prospects that many remote rural landscapes will have social amenities like graded or tarmacked roads, piped water or even electricity.

Despite all the development, Kenya is still home to plenty of untamed hinterland. The private sector has to decentralize for all Kenyans even those in marginal areas to harvest the fruits of devolution. Investing in infrastructure is the single most effective means of devolving the private sector thereby reducing poverty, managing unemployment and staving rural-urban migration among other adverse effects.

Tajiriba Spaces are potentially the most transformative arenas to realize favourable outcomes across Kenya premised on common hopes, mutual benefit and a shared goal thereby connecting every single person and neighborhood to the rest of the world.

CHAPTER FOUR

DEVOLVE DIALOGUE

INTRODUCTION

Citizens should be able to organize and speak up on pertinent issues pertaining to how they are being governed. Citizens should also shape public spending and policy choices. Tajiriba sites and locations are mechanisms for democratizing public participation in governance.

MAKE NEIGHBORHOODS THE FOCUS OF POLICY

The most unattractive aspect of relatedness is that it is responsible for Kenya's decay. Today because of relatedness, neighborhoods are insulated against fresh talent, innovative ideas and fresh thinking that can unlock new experiences, possibilities and deepen the understanding of the world.

Except for opinion polls, civil demonstrations and conflict situations, civilian populations in remote rural locations never get a chance to properly hold public officials to account at the neighborhood, county and national level.

To devolve dialogue, the neighborhood must become the focus of policy. Besides, dialogue must be about shared values and or geography rather than identities. For this to happen, politics should seek to empower geographical locations rather than communities. Relatedness is the reason as to why certain areas remain underdeveloped and freedoms are curtailed.

The world is moving away from neighborhoods dominated by (local exclusionary) communities. Today's' neighborhoods are dominated by people who come from diverse geographical locations. Lineages, clans, ethnicities and other reactionary identities are slowly being phased out of the demographic landscape.

People all over the world are becoming more inclusive in their thinking and attitude towards people that were earlier regarded as outsiders.

Rather than discrimination, competition and hatred along fault lines, connectedness is probably the most important factor influencing policy preferences and choices.

The global village needs three things: a value system, a vision and a clear agenda that goes beyond self-interest. Extended (borderless) neighborhoods can be premised on hope for better days now and tomorrow for the current and future generations.

DECENTRALIZE SCHOLARLY DIALOGUE

Science is a trial and error purposeful process of exploring and making the most of the universe. Relatedness and connectedness are two major approaches for grasping and engaging the universe.

Relatedness represents the old-school approach to focusing and tackling the big issues and questions of society. Connectedness is the contemporary approach in the marketplace of ideas. Connectedness challenges supposed consensus and offers new interpretations to everyday opinions and practices that are frequently take for granted through open debate and discussion.

This undertaking is necessary in order to prod the Kenyan society forward.

Experience suggests that many Kenyans and many people elsewhere cannot or choose not to give up relatedness as long as there is no safer alternative available that is acceptable to them.

Universities and research institutions are centers designed to be populated by the most learned members of society and to provide facilities for instruction, examination, research and application for the benefit of the community of scholars and the wider society.

Sadly, most scholars (the very people who should have a broader viewpoint) have been partisan thereby clueless on the way forward. They have generally embraced relatedness in their scholarly judgments without much thought and as a result Kenyan universities and research institutions have become dens of tribal communes. Universities have not lived up to their mandate as sites of knowledge production, sharing, application and improvements since most scholars remain insular in their thought processes.

The academia has the task of improving partisan politics. Unfortunately, relatedness helps to recruit intellectuals into partisan politics. Without a doubt, the expansion of the Kenyan university system has not helped much to engender democratic tenets, inclusiveness and ideals of shared prosperity. Most Kenyan scholars give integrity to triumphalism (e.g. 'tyranny of numbers') possibly trusting that relatedness is acceptable. This explains why Kenya's politics remains deeply ethnic and myopic.

The academia has failed to guide Kenya on the path of inclusive growth. Unless intellectuals shun relatedness politics, they will continue making minimal contribution to efforts to realize progress, development and technological advancement. Talk of nepotism, clannism, tribalism, ethnic bigotry, negative ethnicity, racism and religious intolerance are mere doublespeak by intellectuals who happen to have a stake in the confusion generated.

Education has failed to unify Kenyans. Scholars are duty bound to participate in public discourse on critical societal issues if they have to make an impact beyond the campus walls. What is lacking here is a mechanism to reason together. It is time for that to change. Frequently whenever relatedness has been successfully used to advance narrow political agendas the unintended consequences have been grave. The public must be engaged by experts whose scholarly judgment is concerned with treating them as a cohesive whole to avoid possible political implosion. To change mindsets, it is necessary to alter the relatedness narrative.

Relatedness has, in many respects, become the curse of our epoch. Relatedness has proved to be exceptionally useful by preventing average citizens from punishing bad governance and rewarding good governance. Relatedness allows self-appointed community spokespersons to pretend to speak for and on behalf of exclusive membership biological groups thereby dragging ordinary into their disgusting selfish pursuits.

Average Kenyan citizens are often victims of misdirected energies thanks to relatedness. Forlornly, prejudice and intolerance have destructive effects on both the perpetrators and victims.

That is why humanity is moving away from vengeful stereotypes, communal self-importance, conflicting territorial claims (boundaries), contested waters, military bases and buildups, national self-determination and spheres of influence. The world is moving away from relatedness and embracing connectedness.

Connectedness marks the beginning of a new era. According to connectedness, scientific and scholarly analysis (expert knowledge) should be about the purpose rather than the method.

Connectedness is conformity with current trends in which the world is shifting away from zero-sum issues based on birthplace, skin colour or lineage toward win-win ones.

Worldwide, governments are spending huge amounts of resources on transport infrastructure to connect neighboring countries and to open new corridors for travel, trade, communication and exchange. For example, the Lamu Port South Sudan Ethiopia Transport Corridor (LAPSSET) is about connecting Kenya, Uganda, Ethiopia, South Sudan and Rwanda. Similarly, the multibillion standard gauge railway project is a key infrastructural initiative at the heart of economic engagement between Kenya, Uganda and Rwanda.

These integrative projects are expected to foster transport linkage between Kenya and other regional states. The projects will also support regional socio-economic development along the different transport corridors.

Remoteness (distance) is no longer a barrier (since contact must not be physical). The Internet is helping to connect people and ideas beyond geographic and time limitations. Facebook, Twitter, Twitter, Google+, You Tube, Instagram, blogs and other disruptive social media spheres have given every individual (millions of users) the platform to directly share positive thoughts, ideas and life events across the globe.

The Internet is now a valuable tool for constructive criticism.

Relatedness is responsible for the spike in hate speech on social media platforms. Relatedness provides the incentive for those who want to misuse digital media spheres to incite communal strife.

Connectedness embraces some (positive) aspects of feminism, socialism and liberalism.

Marxist and feminist thought processes privilege contests along class and gender fault lines but ignores the integrative functions of the workplace and the family. Connectedness is a unifying thought process. According to connectedness, the place of work and the family unit facilitate emotional, social and physical connectedness.

Connectedness agrees with liberalism on individual freedom, free political competition in periodic elections, human rights. Connectedness also subscribes to the assumption by modernization theory that urbanization and (balanced) economic growth can extinguish relatedness.

However, connectedness disavows liberals such as Samuel Huntington who in his 1993 article "The Clash of Civilization" and 1996 book, *The Clash of Civilizations and the Remaking of the World Order*, predicted that the next generation of world conflicts will be the result of a clash of values.

Connectedness also contests Francis Fukuyama's famous (or infamous) formulation that the end of the Cold War (the ideological struggle between liberalism and Communism) meant the ascendancy of Western Civilization (Fukuyama, 1992). In this day and age, the ideological identification with either the left or the right has waned or become redundant.

According to connectedness, globalization thrives on relatedness. Connectedness is the alternative to globalization and other forms of imperialism.

The aforementioned scholars, Huntington and Fukuyama, conveniently ignore objectivity to promote agendas that contradict connectedness.

The second part of Fukuyama's book investigated the shape of a post-historical society and made a disturbing discovery. In a world where the great questions have been solved and geopolitics has been subordinated to economics, humanity will look a lot like the nihilistic "last man" described by the philosopher Friedrich Nietzsche. Human beings will become empty and conceited consumers lacking any meaningful engagement with the world around them.

Nietzsche and Fukuyama did not realize that the human story is the search for meaning. People need to know why they are here (the meaning of existence) for them to prosper. The secret to a meaningful life is discovering one's role in society and assisting others to fruitfully use their adaptive capacities.

According to connectedness, all events and experiences (including struggles in the human society) are driven by the quest to sustain life. Connectedness is incredibly effective in providing solutions to sub-optimal outcomes. To promote achieve connectedness it is imperative to change the neighborhood.

As science grapples with everyday phenomena it can't be divorced from the experiences of ordinary people at the grassroots. Therefore, there is need to devolve universities, research institutes and other scholarly to reach remote rural locations.

CONCLUSION

The entire point of decentralizing scholarly dialogue is to give Kenyans living in informal settlements in urban centers and residents of neighborhoods the opportunity to share their point of view and to be exposed to different experiences, ideas and worldviews in a bid to end polarization, competition and discrimination along fault lines. Without fault lines as envisaged by connectedness, and guided by a common value system, most likely, it is possible for all Kenyans to be able to objectively agree or disagree on public spending, policy choices and how people vote.

CHAPTER FOUR

RESHAPING KENYA'S POLITICAL SPACE

INTRODUCTION

The world is experiencing increased global connectivity and togetherness necessitating a rethink of Kenya's politics. Relatedness is still robustly rooted in Kenya. Most Kenyans still continue to maintain their distinct ethno-linguistic cum political structures and identities (lineages, clans, ethnic groups, races and religious persuasions). Because of relatedness, instead of politics of consensus building and national integration, we frequently witness politics of acrimony.

Kenya is a country well-endowed with natural resources. Yet five decades after attaining self-government, the country is still grappling with distributional grievances along fault lines. In the light of the current unmanageable unemployment levels, soaring poverty and inequality gap, persistent food deficiency and deficient infrastructure, it is vital relegate relatedness to the sidelines.

Public resource allocation is a political undertaking. Remote rural spaces and urban slums (commonly referred to as grassroots) significantly influence Kenya's fragmented politics. Most remote parts of Kenya reasonably feel neglected and alienated by successive governments through skewed socio-economic policies and development blueprints, political patronage, punitive laws, punitive laws, and institutional malpractices.

Kenya's politics is unlikely to change overnight but the world is entering a new phase. Remote rural locations and urban slums can be made the next growth frontier. Conventionally, rural areas are considered bastions of relatedness, while urban areas are more inclined to connectedness. By urbanizing remote rural neighborhoods and urban slums it is possible to enhance connectedness, actualize synergetic democracy and intensify social integration throughout Kenya.

KENYA'S POLITICAL HISTORY

Introduction

The history of Kenya can be divided into three main parts: (a) pre-history; (b) the pre-colonial period; (c) colonial period; (d) the post-colonial or independent period; and (e) broken connectedness period.

Pre-history of Kenya (6,500,000 BCE - 50,000 BCE)

Kenya is reputed to be the site of human origin, the cradle of humankind as evidenced by fossilized remains of ancient hominids. Tools of history (oral tradition, archeology, linguistics, anthropology, genetic research and historical analysis) reveal the presence of humankind in Kenya from as early as the Stone Age.

Christopher Ehret, a linguist, documented the possibility of the ancestors of every human being alive on earth today having lived in the eastern side of Africa at some point in the distant past.

Early humans found in Kenya include Orrorin tugenensis, named after the Tugen Hills and Australopithecus anamensis following a series of fossil discoveries near Lake Turkana.

Remarkable prehistoric sites include Koobi Fora, Tugen Hills, Kariandusi, Namoratunga, Olorgesailie and the walled settlement of ThimLich Ohinga.

Early tools in Kenya include the Oldowan and Acheulian hand axes, picks and flaxes at Kariandusi and Kokiselei in the Rift Valley.

From 500 BCE, Kenya was a migratory path, which saw the arrival of migrants from Africa and the Middle East.

Pre-Colonial Kenya (50,000 BCE – 1885 CE)

Early Settlers

The political history of pre-colonial Kenya is rich and diverse. Present-day Kenya's early settlers (50,000 BCE - 500 BCE) were hunter-gatherer groups learning how to make tools, communicate and use fire.

Evolution of Kenyan Societies

From 500 BCE onwards, the hunter-gatherers were joined by Cushitic language-speaking people (Southern Cushites) from northern Africa (particularly Ethiopia). Cushites speak Afro-Asiatic languages and are divided into two groups: the Southern Cushites and Eastern Cushites.

During the first millennium BCE or the early centuries CE, Bantu and Nilotic speaking people moved into Kenya.

The Bantu speak South-Central Niger-Congo languages. There exist two versions explaining the origin of the Bantu. The first version states that the Bantu came from the Niger Basin (West Africa around the Cameroon Highlands and Baunchi plateau of Nigeria). The second version posits that the Bantu came from the Katanga region in Southeastern Congo.

Nilotes speak Nilo-Saharan languages, and came to Kenya by way of Southern Sudan during the first millennium CE (specifically 500 BCE). Kenyan Nilotes are divided into three main groups: (a) The Highland Nilotes; (b) Plain Nilotes; and (c) River-Lake Nilotes

The other Kenyan language groups include Arabs and the Swahili. The Swahili people (language group) are the product of the intermarriage between the Bantu and Arab/Persian traders.

The Swahili Coast (500 – 1498 CE)

The Swahili Coast shaped up from 500 CE to around 1498 CE. Arab and Persian traders/migrants from the Persian Gulf, southern India and Indonesia began frequenting the Kenya coast around the first century (500 CE) given Kenya's proximity to the Arabian Peninsula.

Arabs from Oman defeated the Portuguese in 1698 CE and took control over Fort Jesus. Through Omani domination (1698-1837), Coastal Kenya came under the sway of Omani Arab traders who established trading posts inspiring Arab and Persian settlements along the coast by the eighth century. These trading posts dealing in ivory and slave trade were directly managed and monopolized by the Sultan of Zanzibar. Seyyid Said, the Oman sultan, had moved his capital from Muscat to Zanzibar.

The Swahili coast remained under the rulership of Muscat until 1837 when the Omanis were finally defeated by the British and the Germans.

The Swahili language, a mixture of Bantu and Arabic, developed as a lingua franca for trade and interaction in a number of coastal towns, notably Pate, Malindi and Mombasa.

A part from Cushitic, Nilotic, Bantu, Arabic and Swahili speakers, Kenya is also inhabited by European and Indian speaking populations.

Portuguese Rule (1498-1698 CE)

The Portuguese were the first Europeans to explore the region of current-day Kenya. The Portuguese navigator Vasco da Gama landed in Mombasa in 1498. The goal of Portuguese presence was not settlement but the establishment of naval bases that would give Portugal control of the Indian Ocean.

Vasco da Gama's voyage was successful in reaching India thereby permitting the Portuguese to trade with the Far East directly by sea. The Port of Mombasa became an important resupply stop for Portuguese ships bound for the Far East. The Arab dominance on the coast was clipped. The Portuguese subsequently ruled the coast for two centuries (1498-1698). They built Mombasa's Fort Jesus as their military headquarters in 1593.

European Exploration in Interior of Kenya (1844 – 1892 CE)

By 1850, European explorers had begun mapping the interior. In 1844, Johann Ludwig Krapf and Johannes Rebmann, became the earliest Europeans to venture into the Kenyan interior. They were followed by Richard Burton and John Speke; and Dr David Livingstone and Henry Stanley, all of whom came to Kenya in search of the source of the Nile. Other

European explorers included Joseph Thomson, James Hannington, Count Samuel Teleki and Ludwig von Hohnel.

Dr. Johann Ludwig Krapf founded the first Christian mission at Rabai in 1846. He later translated the Bible into Swahili.

Production, Exchange and Consumption in Pre-Colonial Kenya

People in pre-colonial Kenya were engaged in hunting and gathering, agriculture, fishing, livestock production, mining and simple manufacturing. The important crafts were blacksmithing, pottery, basketry, woodworking (e.g. the manufacture of drums), and weaving. Crafts were passed down patrilineally in some clans through apprenticeship. People traded with one another.

Prior to colonization, land was inherited patrilineally. A man apportioned his land to sons after they marry but could not alienate the land to daughters. Women had use rights on their husbands' farms but could not inherit land. Mothers could, however, hold land in trust for sons. When his mother died, the last-born son would inherit the land she farmed. Traditionally, one did not own land individually. Communal lands, such as surplus lands or those used for grazing, were under the control of the clan and administered by the clan. Communal grazing lands were common.

In the pre-colonial period (all Kenya groups except the Wanga were acephalous in nature (meaning they had governments, mainly represented by council of elders but they had no centralized governments in place). It is only the Wanga who had a centralized system with Nabongo (meaning King) as their leader.

Kenya's Colonial History (1885-1963 CE)

Berlin Conference and Company Rule (1885 – 1895)

The colonial history of Kenya dates from the Berlin Conference of 1885, when the European powers first partitioned East Africa into spheres of influence. Initially, the British government was reluctant to take active responsibility for the region of east Africa, its acknowledged sphere of interest. The Imperial British East Africa Company, a commercial concern, was tasked to manage this territory on behalf of Britain.

In 1885, German established a protectorate over the Sultan of Zanzibar's coastal possessions, a 10-mile (16-km)-wide strip of land along the coast. In 1890, Germany handed over its coastal holdings (the coastal strip) to Britain to forestall imperial rivalry.

IBEAC administered the current Kenya from 1888 to 1895. In 1895, the company's charter was revoked and the company compensated following severe financial difficulties.

British East Africa Protectorate (1895-1920)

In 1895, Kenya was proclaimed the British East Africa Protectorate by the British Government. This marked the beginning of direct rule and the opening the fertile highlands to white settlers. Schemes were introduced allowing landless aristocrats, middle-class adventurers, big-game hunters, ex-servicemen and Afrikaners to buy land at advantageous rates. By 1915, the majority of fertile highlands in Kenya became the property of the British who practiced a systematic policy of racial segregation.

The East African Protectorate (1895-1920) claimed the interior of Kenya as far west as Lake Naivasha. The border was extended to Uganda in 1902.

Europeans brought thousands of Indians (approximately 32,000) into Kenya to work on building the Kenya Uganda Railway Line. The Kenya-Uganda railway was constructed from 1895 to 1901 to link Mombasa with the British protectorate of Uganda to open up the interior to European settlers, missionaries and administrators, among other colonial activities.

Most of the Indian workers who were brought from British India to do the manual labour during the railway construction decided to stay. They also invited their siblings (Indian traders and businessmen) to join them to exploit the many opportunities in the interior of Kenya.

In 1907, European settlers were accorded voice in government through the Legislative Council. European settlers were the only ones sanctioned to hold elective and appointed positions. The government appointed a European to represent African interests on the Council. Non-Europeans were prohibited from direct political participation until 1944.

Kenya Colony (1920-1963 CE)

European settlers lobbied to transform Kenya into crown colony for them to acquire more influence. In 1920, the East African Protectorate became a crown colony. Kenya Colony was to last from 1920 to 1963.

Why the British Colonized Kenya

Britain established a colony in Kenya provoked by:-

(a) Economic Motives

i.   Need for natural resources and/or cheap raw materials

The forces of industrialization caused European countries to begin looking outside of their borders for cheaper and more abundant raw materials.

ii.   Desire to expand markets (i.e. advantageous markets)

Foreign populations were also viewed as vast markets where goods produced in domestic factories could be sold.

iii. Desire to invest profits

iv.   Outlet needed for growing population

The temperate climate and fertile land in the Kenya highlands was an attraction for European settlement.

v.   Industrial revolution in Britain

Abundant raw materials and vast markets for finished goods are needed in order to maintain an industrialized economy.

(b) Social Motives

i.   Desire to spread Christianity

ii.   Desire to allow European civilization

Europeans viewed the culture of the native population to be inferior to their own. European's sense of superiority made them feel obligated to civilize savage native populations that they encountered in foreign lands. This perception became known as 'The White Man's Burden' after a popular poem by the same name was published by Rudyard Kipling in 1899.

iii.   Belief in social Darwinism

This is the belief that all human groups compete for survival, and that the stronger groups will replace the weaker groups.

iv.   Increased European self-confidence

European nations wanted to demonstrate their power and prestige to the world.

(c) Political and Military Motives

i.   Bases needed for merchant and naval vessels

ii.   National security

Kenya was a military base for the British during the First World War (1914–1918). The Carrier Corps was formed and ultimately mobilized over 400,000 non-Europeans to participate in the war on the side of Britain.

Kenya was again a vital military base for successful campaigns against Italy in the Italian Somaliland and Ethiopia during the Second World War (1939–45).

iii.   Nationalism

Nationalism, or pride in one's country, also contributed to the growth of imperialism. British citizens were proud of their country's accomplishments, which sometimes included taking over foreign areas.

iv.   Balance of power

Britain was forced to acquire new colonies to achieve a balance with her neighbors and competitors (France, Germany and Portugal).

v. Prestige of global empire

As European nations became competitive with one another, there was an increased pressure to practice colonialism in order to maintain a balance of power in Europe.

vi.   Strategic considerations

Britain sought to safeguard and control the Nile, which is the lifeline of Egypt.

British sought to safeguard the interest of British explorers, missionaries, traders and fortune seekers thereby enhance commerce and trade.

(d) Technological Motives

i.   Medical knowledge

ii.   Advances in weapons

iii.   Advances in overseas travel

(e) Industrial Motives

The Industrial Revolution in Britain created an insatiable demand for raw materials and new markets for manufactured goods in order to realize profit.

Main Characteristics of Colonialism

Colonialism (1885 – 1963) thrived on primitive accumulation (land alienation and forced labour) and through exploitative wage labour (Leys, 1975). Generally colonialism in Kenya had the following features:-

(a) Land alienation

Land was taken away from natives for use by European settlers and the colonial administration.

81

Colonial policy and legislation on land tenure barefacedly favored the settlers. Non-Europeans were now formally dispossessed of their land and confined in reserves while settlers were allowed access and ownership of the best farming land.

(b) The settler economy

The settlers banned the growing of coffee, introduced a hut tax, and the landless were granted less and less land in exchange for their labour. A massive exodus to the cities ensued as their ability to provide a living from the land dwindled.

(c) Monetary Economy

Monetary currency was introduced in Kenya during the colonial period. Customarily barter trade was the norm. From the time monetary economy was introduced Kenya became linked to the world capitalist economy.

(d) Wage labour

Settlers needed labour to work on plantations and in their homes as gardeners and or cooks. Administrators also needed cheap (poorly paid) or free non-European labour for public works (e.g. road construction and for buildings).

Indians were brought to build the railway without pay (free labour).

(e) Taxation

Poll and hut tax were introduced. All non-European male over 18 years paid a hut tax and over 16 years a poll tax. Taxation was the main source of revenue. Taxation made it easier for British administrators to run the colony.

(f) Forced labour

Forced labour was the backbone of the colonial economy and colonial administration (e.g. used in First and Second World War). Taxation was a strategy to forcibly acquire the unwilling non-European labour since tax could only be paid using rupees.

(g) Infrastructure and social amenities

Under British direction, roads were built and various systems of transportation (railroad, etc.) and communication (mail, etc.) were put in place.

Social Amenities such as education, sanitation and health facilities were also introduced but they were initially for meant to benefit European settlers.

A railway line was constructed to link Kenya and Uganda. However, the railway was only constructed in Kenya's arable areas where there was economic potential. The railway was therefore meant to make it possible for settlers to exploit Kenya's resources to benefit Britain.

(h) The unitary state and loss of local government

The British government introduced a centralized system of government in Kenya.

New boundaries were imposed bring together communities that in the past existed separately.

The traditional family and village life were transformed.

Punitive expeditions were regularly conducted to subdue and conquer Kenyan language groups that opposed colonialism or colonial exploitation.

(i) Boundaries

Colonialists introduced administrative boundaries based on ethno-linguistic units for their own administrative expediency. The drawing of boundaries somewhat mirrored indigenous ethnic and linguistic groups" namely Bantu, Nilotic and Cushitic. Non-indigenous communities included Arabs, Europeans and Asians.

(j) The urban-rural divide

Nationalism and the Decolonization Process

National self-determination is the idea that every people should get its own state with clearly defined borders. The experience of non-Europeans in the European-settler-dominated Kenya Crown Colony coupled with WWI and WWII experiences gave rise to considerable political activity in the 1920s and after that. Initially nationalist struggles were for reforms but later culminated into struggles for independence.

Nationalism in the context of Kenya in the original sense referred to the process of uniting and regaining freedom from European rule. It was the agitation for independence from the perils of colonialism. Nationalism later came to mean the establishment of a new sovereign country, Kenya, as well as shepherding Kenya's social, economic and political transformation.

Factors Responsible for the Rise of Nationalism in Kenya

The following local, continental and international factors contributed to the rise of nationalism in Kenya, namely:-

Local

(i)   Colonial Policies

The colonial policies led to the growth of nationalism. Evils of colonialism such as forced labor, over taxation, land alienation, racial discrimination and the ban on growing of cash crops etc. made the people to hate the colonial masters.

(ii)   The rise of political consciousness

Non-European Kenyans became increasingly restive and politically conscious and expressed their displeasure with colonial rule through the formation of political parties, resistance movements and in numerous protests, rallies and incidents of violence targeting the colonial regime.

(iii)   The war experience

Though most of the non-British conscriptions during WWI performed ancillary duties such as porting many of them participated in military combat. The experience of these veterans having fought alongside British soldiers gave them a sense pride and self-confidence. They witnessed firsthand British weaknesses and their experiences resulted in the breakdown of the myth of colonial invincibility thereby promoting the anti-colonial drive.

World War II experience further exacerbated the divide between the colonizer and the colonized in Kenya. During the war, the King's African Rifles (KAR) fought heroically in Ethiopia and Burma but returned to Kenya to find that land and recognition was only being accorded to British soldiers in recognition of their services.

Moreover, some of the porters and soldiers conscripted into the King's African Rifles (KAR) did not survive the sojourn; returnees were intensely affected by the experience.

(iv)   Education

The few Kenyans who went to schools acquired a common language – English. This made communication very easy between different language speakers.

(v)   Emergence of urban centers

Towns such as Nairobi, Mombasa, Kisumu, etc emerged. The rapid urban growth and acculturation of Kenyans into urban society (as opposed to relationships along lineage, clan, ethnic and religious common in rural areas) created a conscious mass audience.

(vi)   The rise of charismatic leaders

The rise of able and charismatic leaders such as Jomo Kenyatta, Jaramogi Oginga Odinga, Tom Mboya, and others who organized and led the masses in popular demonstrations and rallies demanding for independence helped nationalist cause.

(vii)   The development of the press

(viii)   The MAU MAU uprising

The Mau Mau rebellion against British rule lasted from 1952 to 56 with the capture of Dedan Kimathi. The uprising took the form of a guerilla war. Kenya was put under a state of emergency from October 1952 to December 1959 and thousands of Kenyans were incarcerated in detention camps. British policymakers sought to isolate the insurgents and their supporters by allowing the participation of non-Europeans in the political process. In 1954, non-Europeans were admitted into the Kenya Legislative Council on a representative basis.

The Mau Mau rebellion prompted the colonists to rethink their colonial policy. In fact, colonial holdings became a burden to maintain. After the state of emergency was lifted in 1960, non- Europeans were given the majority of seats in the legislative council and political parties were formed to take part in the developing political process.

Continental

The 1945 Manchester Pan African conference helped Kenyan nationalism. Delegates including Kwame Nkrumah etc supported the use of all means to defeat colonialism.

(i) World War II

The Second World War weakened the European powers substantially after suffering immense material and manpower loss during the war. Maintaining the Britain Empire became financially and emotionally strenuous. The perception of colonialism changed from being a source of pride to a sense of embarrassment. Many British citizens lost their will to maintain imperial overextend.

(ii) The rise of two new super powers in the world

The Post-war world was also characterized by a new international climate hostile to colonialism. During this period, the United States and the Soviet Union rose to world preeminence. The two powers were opposed European colonies though for different reasons. USA and USSR started supporting ideologically competing political parties struggling for independence. They in the process contributed to the faltering of the European colonial system.

The US viewed the colonies as economic spheres of influence which provided assured markets for former imperial powers' goods. As long as empires existed American businessmen could never to access the market in those colonies. Thus the US had every reason to pressure her allies to decolonize their empires in Asia and Africa.

The USSR also consistently criticized the concept of colonialism arguing it was a harmful practice as it was aimed at economic exploitation of the subject peoples. They argued that colonialism was part and parcel of capitalism which would ultimately collapse due to the inherent contradictions emanating from the exploitation of the weaker states.

(iii)   The Atlantic Charter

In 1941, the US president Roosevelt and the British prime minister W. Churchill signed the Atlantic charter promising subject peoples the enjoyment of the right of self-determination with the conclusion of the war. The charter therefore heightened the expectation of the ex-soldiers and increased the desire for independence in Kenya and elsewhere.

At the conclusion of the Second World War, Britain was weaker in the global balance of power. Britain sought US support through the Marshal plan and she was now compelled to listen to the USA with regard to granting political independence to her subjects.

(iv)   The creation of the United Nations (UN)

New global institutions such as the UN provided new avenues to challenge colonial rule. The UN was created in 1945. The mandate of UN is to promote international peace and security achievable only when all subjects' peoples enjoy the right of self-determination. The UN provided a forum in which individual colonial powers could be challenged or condemned. The UN put pressure on imperial powers to end colonialism.

(v) The Wind of Change

By 1960, many people had changed their attitudes towards colonialism. The conservative government in Britain made the decision to pull out of Kenya, and preparations for independence began.

The Decolonization Process in Kenya

Decolonization refers to the ruination of colonialism. In 1962, Kenyatta was released from prison. The same year he led Kenya's delegation in the negotiations for independence. Thereafter, the Lancaster House Conference was held in 1963 to lay the foundation for an independent Kenya.

On December 12, 1963, *Madaraka* Day, Kenya was declared independent with Jomo Kenyatta as Kenya's first Prime Minister. The following year, on 12th December 1964 (*Jamhuri* Day), under a new constitution, Kenya became a Republic with Kenyatta as its first President.

At independence, Kenya's territory included the coastal strip which until this time has been leased from the sultan of Zanzibar. The British government bought out the white settlers and they mostly left Kenya.

History of Independent Kenya

Post Independent Kenyan political history can be demarcated into several periods namely: Kenyatta regime (1963-1978); Transition to Moi Regime; The Moi Era (1978-2002); The Kibaki Era (2003-20012; and Uhuru Kenyatta Era (2013-?).

Kenyatta Regime (1963-1978)

Jomo Kenyatta embraced a successful free-market economy and was agreeable to foreign investment. Underlying social tensions were evident, however. Kenya's very rapid population growth rate, considerable rural to urban migration, illiteracy and bad governance (i.e. tribalism, nepotism, cronyism, *de facto* one-party authoritarian state, land grabbing and other forms of corruption) were in large part responsible for poverty, high unemployment and disorder in the cities.

Following Kenyatta's death on 22nd August, 1978 Vice President Daniel Arap Moi became interim and eventually succeeded him as Kenya's second President.

Moi Era (1978 – 2002)

Moi continued in the footsteps of Kenyatta (*Nyayo* philosophy) pursuing free market policies, one-party rule, with minimal acceptance of dissent.

On August 1 1982 air force personnel led by Hezekiah Ochuka and backed by university students, attempted a coup d'état to oust Moi. The coup failed. Moi's reaction was to ruthlessly clamp down on rebellions marking the beginning of despotic rule in Kenya. In June 1982, the National Assembly amended the constitution making Kenya officially (*de jure*) a one-party state.

The 1983 and 1988 elections were held under a single party framework. The way these elections were conducted did meet the minimum threshold for democracy bolstering calls for the return to multi-party politics.

In December 1991, in the face of severe domestic and international pressure and criticism, Moi asked parliament to repeal the one party section (section 2A) paving the way for the re-introduction of political pluralism.

By early 1992, several new parties had formed, and multiparty elections were held in December 1992. Because of divisions in the opposition, however, Moi was reelected for another 5-year term, and his KANU party retained a majority of the legislature.

Parliamentary reforms in November 1997 expanded political space allowing for the formation of more political parties. Again because of a divided opposition, Moi won re-election as President in the December 1997 elections.

Kibaki Era and Grand Coalition (2002-2013)

In October 2002, the National Rainbow Coalition (NARC) was formed, emerging from a unification of opposition parties together with a faction, which broke away from KANU. Mwai Kibaki, the NARC candidate, was elected as the country's third President in December 2002.

During Kibaki's first time in office, democratic space was opened up even more and coalition politics took root. However, Kenya's General Election of 27th of December 2007 degenerated into a month long spate of violence in some parts of the country, leading to loss of lives, dislocation of some citizens, destruction of property, and general disruption of social and economic life. A Grand Coalition was formed bring together the main contenders to stabilize the country.

KENYA'S BROKEN CONNECTEDNESS HISTORY

For millions of years humans have maintained interdependence through mingling, trading and bartering, new settlements, relocation, migration and diverse forms of imperialism that include colonialism.

Today Kenyan inhabitants are grouped into major clusters: (a) the Cushites; (b) the Nilotes; (c) the Bantu; (d) Arabs; (e) Swahili; (f) Europeans; and (g) Indians.

Kenyan language groups (Cushitic, Nilotic, Bantu, Arabic, Swahili, European and Indian speakers) have interacted over the years by way of marriage, trade, politics, education, new settlement patterns and urbanization. However, relatedness still stands tall as a form of identity and belonging. Because of relatedness, Kenya is a country of distinct ethnic territories. Thus, all Kenyans belong to specific lineages, clans, ethnic groups, races and religious persuasions, and they identify with them first and foremost.

Given relatedness, these interactions have also been through conflicts supposedly over scarce resources, mainly land, grazing pasture and water points. Other times the clashes and conflicts have been fueled by politicians to gain political mileage and prestige.

Today the relationships among Kenyans are beset with untold challenges. National cohesion remains an elusive dream. Politicized councils of elders collude with conniving politicians out to cause divisions, tensions and conflicts.

Most scholars blame colonial policies for fomenting current-day ethnic pride, bias and hate. Perhaps, five decades after the end of colonialism, attributing the current day challenges to colonialism distracts us from confronting the real problem, which is relatedness. Relatedness is responsible for slavery, colonialism, globalization, corruption and mismanagement, inequality, impunity and the poor delivery of basic services.

Apparently, Kenya's decolonization process of the 1950s and 1960s was blatantly anti-colonial and or anti-British. Kenyans supported decolonization struggles to undo humiliating colonial occupation but for different motives. Once the colonial powers officially pulled out, the successive Kenyan leaderships that emerged became selfish and were keener to consolidate power and rid themselves of political rivals. Military coup attempts, one-party political systems, widespread corruption, and tyrannical autocrats became the norm.

Relatedness is divisive. Relatedness divides Kenyans into discrete competing units. Five decades after attaining internal self-governance, Kenyans have not managed to put collective interests above regional, ethnic and or religious ones. Ethnic rivalries, diseases, unemployment, globalization, corruption, greed, and natural disasters have decidedly shaped the reality that is post-independence Kenya.

At independence a compromise was reached to divide the country into eight provinces. This move emboldened relatedness. Under the re-organization stipulated by the 2010 constitution, the country's eight provinces were replaced with 47 county administrations.

The 47 counties were created to even the electoral process and address grievances of power and resource distribution after decades of centralized administration (RoK/IRC/ Kriegler and Waki Reports (2008); Kanyinga, Okello, & Akech, 2010; RoK, 2010).

It is strange what relatedness can do. The new constitution has not changed established attitudes and values. Divisions have continued to deepen. Kenyans appear as divided as before. Johann Kriegler, the retired South African Judge, in September 2013 noted that, despite its much acclaimed new constitution, the only "way to save Kenya is by liberating the country from ethnic ideologies".

In Kenya, the centrality of relatedness to political mobilization is well-documented. Relatedness is the most significant determinant of voting patterns. Relatedness can be highly divisive since it influences our political attitudes, values and voter preferences. No wonder, since the re-introduction of multipartisysm every election year (1991/1992; 1997 Likoni clashes; 2007/2008 disputed presidential elections; 2012/2013

Tana Delta clashes) Kenya has witnessed election-related identity conflicts.

Relatedness is a fertile ground for the politics of exclusion, political mobilization of distributional grievances and accountability failure. Devious politicians vying for county, parliamentary and particularly the presidency often resort to forming ethnic alliances and coalitions.

If not timely addressed, relatedness can make the state to lose its capacity to provide goods and service to most of its citizens.

SYNERGETIC DEMOCRACY IN KENYA

Introduction

In Kenya, relatedness often stands in the way of democracy. The 2010 constitution was meant to manage relatedness. Kenyans wanted to chart a new path of connectedness. The Constitution introduced devolution and provided for a bicameral parliament. This seems not to have happened.

For Kenya to be part and parcel of the global connectivity and togetherness movement, it is imperative to fix broken governance to pull off synergetic democracy.

To dismantle relatedness thereby cultivate synergetic democracy in Kenya, it important to uphold value-driven politics; strengthen political parties; encourage inclusive neighborhoods; engage politicians in between elections; cultivate pro-active neighborhood policymaking; and develop neighborhood infrastructure.

Uphold Value-Driven Politics

Politics for the most part deals with participation and representation in decision-making in the process of the allotment of value (Khamala, 2015a).

For thousands of years scientists and practitioners have pondered over how best to allocate value to satisfy the principles of participation, equity and fairness.

Niccolò Machiavelli, a renaissance scholar, in *The Prince* (1532 CE) originated the understanding that value allocation has to do with power and interests. Machiavelli preferred an arrangement where powerful individual(s) in charge of an efficient, responsive and capable state control assets and decision-making.

Machiavelli significantly influenced Thomas Hobbes (1588-1679) who in *Leviathan* advocated for absolutism in statecraft to effectively deal with people's foibles and frailties. However, soon after scholars such as John Locke (632-1704), John Stuart Mill (1806-1873) and Jean-Jacques Rousseau (1712–1778) proposed checks and balances, the general will and a range of limits to executive authority to forestall possible abuse of power.

Machiavellianism appeals to the appalling duplicitous side of humanity. Machiavellianism worship subtle treachery, deceit and bad motives in human affairs in attempts to pursue and maintain state power. That being the case, Machiavellianism epitomizes relatedness. However, Machiavellianism (and by extension relatedness) is now dated. The changes were motivated by the realization that the end does not justify the means in all cases.

Humanity is entering a new world of connectedness. Connectedness embraces love (positive emotion) rather than fear (negative emotion). Nowadays leaders prefer to be loved instead of being feared.

Today, power is negotiated and as such leadership is synergetic and value-laden. The enduring leadership strategy is not one that exploits weaknesses in other people (opportunistic) but one that builds on other people's strengths (team player). Statecraft is embraced mediation, conciliation, arbitration, diplomacy, dialogue, participation, collaboration and consultation.

Synergetic democracy emphasizes value-laden politics. Duplicity and shameless political theatrics have waned in the face of public leadership ethics. Power is not an end; power is the means to a meaningful life.

Institutionalize Political Parties

Synergetic democracy is anchored on issue-driven parties. Democracy thrives when political parties provide policy choices for public benefit since they are platforms from where public opinions are formed; policies formulated; and programmes for prior-agreed-upon policies developed and implemented.

A political party is a group of voters organized to support certain policy options. Political parties stand for alternative policy positions. Each political party stands for a set of policies, mobilizes support for its policy programmes and tries to elect officials to carry out the party's policy platforms.

Basically, political parties facilitate participative politics; provide the means by which citizens can participate in the governance process, and or originate more responsive policies.

Robert Dahl in *Party System and Patterns of Opposition* (1966) classified party systems by counting the number of parties in a polity, namely, one-party system; two-party system; and multi-party systems (where there are more than three parties).

The current understanding of political did not take shape until the late 17th century (1600's).

The Ancient Greeks who pioneered a humanistic outlook, developed democracy and ushered in scientific and rational inquiry, had no organized political parties in the contemporary sense.

The ancient Romans (Greco-Roman) had the Patricians and the Plebeians. The Patricians represented noble families while the Plebeians represented the wealthy merchants and the middle class. The Patricians and the Plebeians mingled but at times they voted as factions (or parties) on particular issues that were important to the groups they represented.

For many centuries after the fall of Rome (476 CE), ordinary people in Europe had modest voice in politics since there were no veritable political parties. What existed were rival cliques and factions that supported particular noble families or influential personalities opposed to one another. Participation in the political process was therefore restricted to princes, dukes, counts, marquises, etc.

Political parties began from the time representative assemblies took shape. The first political parties in Britain began during the reign of Charles II after the Popish Plot of 1678 CE.

In 1678 CE, a rumor spread through England that Roman Catholics were plotting to kill King Charles II (a protestant) and give the throne to his brother James (a Catholic) who was then the Duke of York. Parliament barred all Roman Catholics from public office and tried to take away the Duke of York's right to inherit the throne. But to King Charles II, the legislative assembly seemed to be challenging royal (absolute) authority, and to forestall such an eventuality, he dissolved it.

The King's action paved the way for the participation of ordinary people in politics along alternative policy ideals. The masses were either for (Abhorrers) or against (Petitioners) the king's act. The petitioners wanted the king to call a new legislative body. The abhorrers disliked efforts to control the king's actions. Before long the petitioners were called Whigs while the king's supporters were called Tories.

The basic difference between Whigs and Tories in the 1600's was their view of what government should do and how strong it should be. Tories wanted rule by an unrestrained sovereign. Whigs wanted ordinary people to have more rights and gain more control of their government. In time, as the legislative assembly took greater control, the Whigs and Tories developed into organized parties.

Nascent political parties underwent major transformations in Europe and the United States in the 19th century with the dawn of electoral and parliamentary regimes subsequent to the French and American revolutions. Regimes supported by nobles were succeeded by regimes supported by other elites (merchants, bankers, industrialists, businessmen, etc.). From this period, political parties started to rely on mass support.

The 20th century saw the reach of political parties extending to cover the entire world. The term political party has since come to refer to all organized groups seeking political power, whether through elections or via insurgency.

The story of the origins and evolution of party politics in the context of Africa can be traced the True Whig Party, which was set up in Liberia in 1860. Almost a century later, several nascent political parties were formed by African elites during the colonial period demanding reforms as a strategy to influence colonial policy.

Noticeably, new political parties proliferated on the continent during the final stages of the colonial period, and during the period immediately preceding or after independence in the late 1950s and early 1960s respectively. This is basically because political parties by design fulfill an integrative function. Political parties then were formed and tasked to bring the African people together regardless of their ethno-political affiliation under the banner of getting rid of colonial rule.

Anyang' Nyong'o in *30 years of Independence in Africa* (1992) correctly observes that the people on the continent were categorized into social groups that were historically antagonistic such that they could not be easily be mobilized to collectively confront the colonial regime. In essence political parties in Africa were founded with the goal of being the main vehicles for African Nationalism. The colonized tired of the toils of colonialism gave huge electoral support to the main liberation movements and political parties.

Political parties were vehicles for African Nationalism before independence. However, party pluralism soon proved to be poorly rooted on the continent the moment independence became a reality. In a span of a few years, authoritarian forms of government (one-party states, military regimes, civil dictatorships, etc.) came to prevail practically everywhere on the continent during the decades of the 1960s to 1990s.

Relatedness often dilutes the spirit of synergetic democracy. Evidently, between the 1960s and 1990s popular participation in Africa was stifled by relatedness (lineage, clan, ethnic, regional and or religious cleavages). The African continent failed to institutionalize its political and governance structures to facilitate political participation. Thereafter, democratic systems failed.

The African political elites that controlled independence political parties took advantage of socio-political cleavages to gain power through unmistakably undemocratic means. Political participation (mobilization and organization) was left to occur along pre-existing fault lines rendering societal relations to be highly frail and fractious. Governments came to power (presidency) and or were removed from power by mobilizing sentiments along fault lines.

The justification for the switch to authoritarianisms included the need to concentrate on economic development, the desire to prevent fragmentation along socio-political cleavages and so on.

Even then, this period (1960s to 1990s) witnessed slowed growth, widespread poverty, high indebtedness, foreign-policy missteps, political instability, conflicts and wars, just to mention a few of the plethora of difficulties that plagued African countries.

The dismantling of the Berlin Wall in the late 1980s and the collapse of the former Soviet Union in the early 1990s triggered the resurgence of political pluralism in Africa. During the global third wave of democratization, which raged across the world, virtually all African countries shifted from army-dominated and or single-party-dominated regimes to multiparty systems and practices.

Political liberalization paid dividends and improved the governance process in some parts of Africa. This evidenced by dynamics of the party system landscape that has been witnessed since Kenya's independence.

In the run-up to Kenya's independence two groups emerged: the centralists (championing unitary constitution) and the federalists (championing Majimbo constitution).

Centralists led by the Kenya National African Union (KANU) advocated for a unitary state while federalists led by the Kenya African Democratic Union (KADU) were for federal units. Federalists majorly aimed to protect the interests of minority communities against the numerically populous Kikuyu and Luo communities that comprised the majority of KANU's membership.

KADU (federalists), which participated in the freedom struggle, lost the first general election in 1963. Thereafter, the party dissolved as an opposition party and merged with the then ruling party KANU in 1964. From 1964, Kenya became a de facto one party state.

In 1966, the former vice president of Kenya Jaramogi Oginga Odinga quit KANU and founded the Kenya People's Union (KPU). Odinga in *Not Yet Uhuru* (1968) argued that despite the country's declared self-rule, the independent government in Kenya was as oppressive as the colonial government. KPU was proscribed shortly thereafter and its leader arrested in 1969, detained for two years and subsequently elbowed out of politics until Kenyatta's death in 1978.

Party pluralism and opposition politics from this point on (1969 – 1982) were thwarted discreetly, through intimidation and/or through legislation. For example, after the August 1 1982 coup attempt, the National Assembly altered the constitution, making Kenya a *de jure* (by law) one-party state. The one-party state lasted until 1991 when parliament repealed the one party section (section 2A) paving the way for the re-introduction of party pluralism.

Kenya has held five general elections since the restoration of multiparty democracy in 1991. However, periodic elections are not by themselves a guarantee for synergetic democracy. Kenya's multi-party elections in 1992, 1997, 2002, 2007 and 2013 were marred by proliferation of parties, allegations of ballot-box stuffing, the ethnicisation of politics and targeted ethnic violence (Saidi, 2006; Ongoya, Elisha & Otieno, 2012).

The December 2002 opposition party win was dubbed the NARC Revolution because for the first time in independent Kenyan history, the opposition beat backed by the incumbent based on issues. The NARC policy platform was very attractive; namely, Free Primary Education (FPE); 500 jobs per year; a new constitution in a hundred days; fundamental governance reforms such as zero tolerance to corruption; and a set of promised infrastructure projects.

Kenya's disputed 2007 General Election turned chaotic. Lives were lost, property destroyed and many citizens dislocated. Koffi Annan, the former Secretary General of the United Nations with the assistance of eminent persons from across the African continent under the auspices of the African Union (AU) helped broker a reconciliation culminating with the signing of the National Accord and Reconciliation Agreement. The Agreement included the formation of a Grand Coalition between Mwai Kibaki's Party of National Unity (PNU) and Raila Odinga's Orange Democratic Movement Party (ODM).

The history of Kenya's politics is such that political parties are yet to operate as well-functioning institutions. Parties in Kenya are largely been elitist associations. Subsequently, Kenya's political scene is characterized by overnight mushrooming of briefcase political parties; the lack of internal democracy; party hopping; and the formation of regional parties, ethnic alliances, and coalitions of convenience.

Most political parties are founded purposely as vehicles for specific individuals to ascend to power. The major parties have strong personalities (the party leader and a few of his cronies) around which the party membership revolves. These individuals control, fund or scramble for key positions in political parties so as to influence decisions that further their political careers. The role of the party membership is to endorse decisions already made by the party elite and leadership.

Party hopping and internal democracy are two sides of the same coin. The political class often perceives political parties as vehicles for contesting and attaining public office. Party elites frequently prefer to control party politics through highly centralized and non-inclusive decision-making processes and internal structures of patronage at the expense of the party membership.

Politicians also regularly champion the formation of regional parties to entice Kenyans to vote along lineage, clan, ethnic, religious and race lines. Since independence, Kenya's political arena has tribal coalescing in the form of the Gikuyu, Embu, Meru and Akamba (Gema) association, the Kalenjin, Maasai, Turkana and Samburu (Kamatusa and recently the Luhya,

Teso and Sabaot (Lutesa) association. Related to this is the emergence of the Commonwealth of Coast Counties.

Political parties are supposed to base their political action and program on stated ideological standpoints. In a political sense, an ideology refers to the body of ideas, ideals, principles, doctrines, strategies and or symbols to explain the world while providing a blueprint to change it through political engagement. Typically, each ideology represents a system of certain ideas on what can be considered to be the best way of organizing society politically (e.g. democracy, theocracy, caliphate, feminism, etc.), and the best economic system (e.g. capitalism, socialism, mixed economy, etc.).

Historically the major ideologies include mercantilism; socialism; communism; anarchism; fascism; nationalism; liberalism (classical liberalism, modern liberalism, monetarism, neo-liberalism, and liberal/social democracy); conservatism; and mixed economy.

Some scholars have suggested that Kenyan political parties regularly falter since they are not guided by clear ideologies creating room for the emergence of patronage and clientilist politics.

Institutionalization is the path to strengthening political parties in Kenya. Most political parties in Kenya reflect pre-existing ethno-linguistic cleavages. Because political parties are supposed to be the measure of democratic electoral outcomes it is important for them to inclusive to appeal to a wider membership. This lack of inclusiveness acts as a severe limitation to party mobilization along alternative policy positions. The cure for this mischief is to overcome the overriding influence of relatedness on party politics in Kenya.

Connectedness places a high premium on intra-party democracy, which is critical for party politics. Political parties are the vehicles through citizens get the opportunity to actively participate in the political process. Broad participation in political party decision-making shapes the policy choices that parties ultimately offer to voters.

Broad membership participation also promotes party unity through reduced factionalism and/or fragmentation; creates legitimate internal conflict management systems; structure the political landscape to facilitate dialogue between supposedly contending interests and policy objectives; and reduces opportunistic and arbitrary use of delegated authority.

Expansive membership participation in party organs can take the form of policy formulation, the election of party officials and the nomination of electoral candidates.

Connectedness places a high premium on citizen participation in political processes. Whereas relatedness is about political competition, connectedness (synergetic democracy) is about political participation. A truly participatory model of democracy is one that has strong and credible political parties. Synergetic democracy is based on political participation along alternative party platforms. This way, the membership of political parties exercise some form of control over party leadership, the crafting of policy prescriptions and setting the policy agenda. On this score, political parties act as bridges to surmount deep rooted and pre-existing fault lines and cleavages in their internal organization and decision-making processes.

Encourage Inclusive Neighborhoods

Typically coexistence among Kenyans is the norm in major towns and cities where people intermingle with ease. The same cannot be said of remote rural locations and/or urban slums. Discrimination and the consequent sense of alienation largely contribute to the sustained neglect of remote rural locations and informal settlements.

Political instigation along fault lines is responsible for suspicion, disunity and discord among Kenyans. The probability of the occurrence of violent conflicts in Kenya increase the moment political contests mirror ethnic cleavages and long- standing inter-ethnic animosities accompanied by distributional grievances.

The framers of the 2010 Constitutional dispensation realigned Kenya's political map to allow free movement and residence for all Kenyans with roots in other geographical areas. In fact, according to contemporary laws any person born in Kenya (even of non-Kenyan parents) automatically becomes a Kenyan citizen. However, politicians are known for balkanizing the country through their utterances, actions and political zonal.

The world is witnessing an emerging universal worldview. Connectedness transcends the present paradigms of identities, demarcations, and borders. Connectedness does away with borders instead of redrawing them. With connectedness, people don't have to choose neighbors, who to do business with, and where to buy property. Through inclusive neighborhoods, Tajiriba Spaces, it is possible to eliminate the current portrayal of people as non-locals, outsiders and/or intruders.

Engage Politicians In Between Elections

Democratic governments are run by political parties. In democracies the power to lead is attained via electoral means. Political parties attempt to convince electors to be given the opportunity to implement their policy prescriptions. Voters express their preference by voting for the candidates that most closely reflect their views. Unfortunately, political parties in Kenya lack political programmes beyond elections. Citizens properly engage political parties in between elections when they have post-polls programmes.

Cultivate Pro-Active Neighborhood Policymaking

Kenya's development strategy and policies must be equipped with effective redistributive mechanisms. This is because current strategies and policies promote the heavy concentration of value among high-income elite and in major towns and cities thereby contributing to a high degree of income inequality. Subsequent economic growth tends to perpetuate and intensify these inequalities.

It is on record that successive governments have at one time or the other pursued skewed public policy frameworks. For example, Sessional Paper No. 10 of 1965 prioritized development and investment in 'high potential regions' thereby consigning the 'unproductive' arid and semi-arid regions into economic oblivion. The legacy was grinding poverty and underdevelopment.

To stimulate economic productivity and growth, we have had the NARC Government's Economic Recovery Strategy for Wealth and Employment Creation (ERS), the creation of the National Social and Economic Council (NESC) and Kenya Vision 2030.

The Jubilee government has prioritized a plethora of mega-projects in energy and infrastructure to reduce the cost of production, grow the economy, transform the country into a middle-income level state and pull the mass of Kenya's poor out of poverty. The Kenya government has also initiated a set of programmes such as the Youth Enterprise Development Fund, UWEZO Fund and affirmative action.

The devolution component was expected to end the perennial problem of distributional grievances behind the 2008 post-election violence.

All these initiatives may amount to nothing with pro-active citizen participation in initiation, design, execution, monitory and evaluation of policymaking. Pro-active neighborhood policymaking is necessary to enhance equalization of development in all parts of the country.

Neighborhood Infrastructure

The pattern of government income and expenditure, the fiscal and tax system and investment policy determine the fairness of the value allocation process. By failing to invest sufficiently in all parts of the country particularly in remote rural environments and informal settlements, the inequality gap continues to grow every year. Inequities when wide enough tend to spur tensions and divisions.

Kenya's Vision 2030 recognizes infrastructure as an important enabler for sustained economic growth. The country cannot achieve Vision 2030 unless infrastructural deficits and the accompanying income distribution are corrected. Tajiriba

Spaces are meant to ensure that all regions are given a fair share of goods, services and infrastructure to facilitate seamless connectivity to the rest of the country and the world.

Rewarding Excellence

Every Kenyan has the capacity for achievement, success and development. Success depends on fate, luck, hard work, persistent optimism and the goodwill of others. Today, many Kenyans (including millennials) are focused on using their talents to make the world a better place. They value social impact and growth opportunities. Unfortunately, Kenya is slowly growing into a society that does not honor honest pursuit of wealth and influence. Tajiriba Spaces are avenues to celebrate holidays, special events, and people who are trying to make a difference.

CONCLUSION

In this day and age, instead of the usual politicking (divide and rule approach) it is timely to explore synergetic democracy to diversify the economy in order to exploit Kenya's untapped resources.

CHAPTER FIVE

A KENYA WITH A CONNECTEDNESS FACE

INTRODUCTION

The Kenya Government is constitutionally mandated to protect lives, secure property rights and provide basic services.

Every Kenyan wants security, affordable cost of living and a stable source of income. Quite the reverse; current policies have driven the cost of living well beyond the means of ordinary Kenyans. The population of Kenyans without stable sources of income is growing faster than the country's ability to generate or expand income opportunities.

For a long time, many Kenyans have expected the government to solve the unemployment problem with minimal input from ordinary citizens. However, creating adequate income opportunities requires long-term vision, commitment and proactive participation by average citizens especially in the face of rising public expenditure, government ineptitude, corruption and unfulfilled election promises.

Relatedness frequently comes in handy to conceal mediocrity, improper management of public funds and poor governance. Relatedness thrives on divide-and-rule tactics as it engenders a sense of triumphalism in some sections of the society and a sense of insecurity, exclusion and underrepresentation in others.

Relatedness is the handiest weapon for those hell bent on inciting communities to violence. Relatedness has also been the subject of much criticism and ridicule because it allows for upward mobility based on patronage, rather than experience and merit.

Relatedness also prevents the private sector from taking advantage of numerous investment opportunities in Kenya especially those in remote rural locations and urban slums.

Relatedness is a daunting and complex multi-pronged challenge that frequently results in unsatisfactory outcomes. Kenya's economy cannot grow in an environment characterized by division, suspicion and hatred.

Little wonder, the underlying mechanisms of relatedness tend towards lack of adequate income opportunities for everyone and thereby massive inequality. Besides, democratic institutions cannot work properly if inequity becomes too extreme and in an environment characterized my suspicion, distrust and hate.

In fact, many hard-up Kenyans without stable income opportunities may be tempted to run the risk to their lives to put food on the table or to simply destroy any gains made thus far.

A Kenya with a connectedness face typifies the growth of affluence without the accompanying concentrations of joblessness, poverty and inequity.

Connectedness is the solution to the current reality where more and more wealth is being concentrated in the hands of fewer and fewer people.

Prosperity in remote geographical locations and informal settlements is achievable with proper planning, prudent investment and the necessary synergy. This means transforming the way ordinary Kenyans relate with each other and elected national and county government leaders.

Through Tajiriba Spaces, it is possible to manage the schism among Kenyans and the economic and social inequalities that relatedness produces and to create new pathways for opportunity in order to uplift and secure the lives of most Kenyans.

The idea of Tajiriba Spaces is the most unlikely intervention strategy to realizing better economic prospects or a Kenya with a connectedness face. However, because governments often intimidate, cajole and even discriminate against their own populations and geographical locations, alternative mechanisms must be found to countermand uneven development.

Kenya's double-digit economic growth aspiration appears overly optimistic unless Kenyans agree to share existing benefits more widely. The focus is to ensure that almost everyone in Kenya actively contributes to the overall growth of the country. No Kenyan should feel favored or discriminated against by their government for whatever reason.

Urbanized neighborhoods, Tajiriba Spaces, are innovative mechanisms to support Kenya's progression to a high-income country with a target growth rate of 10 per cent or more. Offerings at Tajiriba Spaces are aligned to the letter and spirit of the 2010 Constitution, Kenya's long-term development agenda commonly known as Vision 2030, the Jubilee Manifesto, the CORD manifesto and other policy documents.

If implemented, this plan can support and strengthen devolved governments, improve service delivery and grow the number of Kenyans with disposable income to spend and move close to 9 million people out of entrenched poverty. The project can also bolster the country's revenue collection of Sh900 billion to almost 4 trillion annually by the year 2025.

IMPLIMENTATION PHASES

Tajiriba Spaces are founded on the realization that as individuals we are extended and as such we frequently worry about our mission in life, our legacy. We aspire to touch lives, reach out and make a difference in our natural and social surroundings through investments in anticipation of better social and financial returns (private sector), through the provision of public goods and service (governments), and/or through charitable causes (non-profit mechanisms).

Model Neighborhoods

In the initial phase, each county will have a model Tajiriba Space. In addition, each remote rural location (Mt Elgon, Turkana, Pokot, Samburu, Mfangano, and Rusinga islands, among others) and each border point (Lwakhakha, Sio Port, Loitoktok, Namanga, Isebania, Taveta, Lungalunga, Vanga, Malaba, Busia, Liboi, Mandera/Elwak, Moyale, Lokichogio and Dif) will also have a Tajiriba Space.

Iconic Neighborhoods

Iconic villages will be dedicated to honoring, acknowledging, rewarding and celebrating past and current heroes and heroines, exemplary leadership, excellence, enterprise, creativity, innovation and talent.

Through Tajiriba Spaces, it is possible to provide platforms for acknowledging outstanding accomplishments. It is time to devise a new way of honoring human achievements. Instead of erecting statues and building monuments, it is wise to promote connectedness by touching peoples' lives and changing landscapes.

Charity begins at home. Invest in your neighborhood to change society. If you elect someone to public office you change a life but if you invest in the neighborhood you transform lives. The bottom line is that investing in your neighborhood has a great rate of return for the future.

This is also an opportunity to pay homage to a neighborhood that has left a long-lasting impression in one's life. It could be the neighborhood where one was born or raised. It could also be one's current residence or workplace. It could also be a neighborhood one spent part of their childhood, youth or adulthood. It could also be a neighborhood one visited at some point in their life and they were touched by poverty levels, terrain, hospitality or ambience, among other reasons.

FUNDING

Tajiriba Foundation intends to fundraise over Khs 530 billion to construct and manage 517 Tajiriba Spaces in remote rural locations and urban slums across the country inside 10 years. The funds will be raised manly by public and private donations from individuals, corporate organizations, charitable organizations, trusts, foundations, governments and other donors. Other sources will include equity and types of loans from local and international financial institutions. Volunteers will also be able to donate their time, artworks, materials and services.

The foundation will partner with spouses of presidential candidates, governors and senators after every election year to promote and fund Tajiriba Spaces. The foundation will also work with top politicians; distinguished scholars; media personalities; successful entrepreneurs; top businesspeople; musicians; artists; human right activists and ordinary Kenyans to market and fundraise for Tajiriba Spaces.

The foundation will also partner with the private sector and other interested parties to jointly promote and fund some of its flagship projects on profitable and commercial terms.

On this score, some of the funding may come from county governments, which are permitted by law to invest a maximum of Sh250 million for such ventures.

Other sources may include the state-run pension fund National Social Security Fund (NSSF), trade unions under the umbrella of the Central Organization of Trade Unions

(COTU), independent associations and employer organizations such as Federation of Kenya Employers (FKE).

The foundation hope to partner with the Unclaimed Financial Assets Authority (UFAA), the custodian of unclaimed financial assets that include money left in bank accounts that have since been dormant for some time, retirement benefits, dividends and matured insurance policies. According to a 2008 report compiled by a Treasury appointed taskforce unclaimed assets amounts to approximately Kshs. 9 billion. These assets can be put to good use before they are reunited with their owners or next of kin.

In the fullness of time the organization will become self-sufficient financially.

THE CONCEPT

Tajiriba means "experience" in Swahili. Tajiriba Spaces (urbanized village arenas) are free public places originated and managed by Tajiriba Foundation for public benefit on non-profit making basis. These are innovative mechanisms to make possible individual and private enterprise (private sector) in remote rural locations and urban slums.

Tajariba spaces represent an innovative avenue to redress unemployment, rural-urban migration, infrastructural deficits and historical and contemporary neglect characteristic of remote rural geographical locations and urban slums around the world.

Through Tajiriba Spaces it is possible to comprehensively devolve and facilitate the penetration of the private sector to all parts of the world. Urbanized neighborhoods also envision political reforms, even economic development and sustainable social change.

Through Tajiriba Spaces it is also possible to facilitate as many people as possible to leave an indelible mark on the universe.

Through Tajiriba Spaces it is possible to shape policy discourse, mobilize resources, generate more than 9 million income opportunities, improve livelihoods and develop infrastructure in rural remote environments and informal settlements to facilitate inclusive growth.

THE ORGANIZATION

Tajiriba Foundation is an independent non-profit start-up organization that is pioneering the most distinctive and unlikely thought process (Connectedness) from the most improbable source, that may radically change our place and understanding of the universe, and whose application (Tajiriba Spaces) represents another significant stride in the human hunt for meaning.

Human interaction and contact based on relatedness emphasizes exclusive political formations, boundaries, divisions, discrimination, competition and win-lose or lose-lose scenarios. As expected, relatedness leads to constant struggles and conflicts, war scenarios, insufficient employment and widespread poverty. Alternatively, connectedness emphasizes values, fairness, justice, equality and inclusiveness.

The organization seeks to grow the private sector in remote rural locations and informal settlements through Tajiriba Spaces among other signature projects to manage unemployment, advance equality of opportunity, promote inclusive development and better governance, reduce poverty and injustice, safeguard democratic values, promote international cooperation and good relations among ordinary citizens and neighborhoods, and advance a greater role for the nonprofit sector.

To achieve the stated objective, the organization targets to raise Kshs. 530 billion from various sources of funding, including high net worth individuals, development finance institutions, local and foreign institutional investors and pension funds. Alternative sources of funding may also include unclaimed assets.

Venture capitalists and strategic investors can also partner with the foundation to profit from village ads (Tajiriba Ads), neighborhood tourism (Tajiriba Tours & Travel) and Tajiriba conferencing.

The organization also hopes to originate and spread scientific knowledge in a way that is accessible to all to help build a cohesive humanity.

The foundation is not a charitable organization. Neither is it an employment agency.

As part of the more than Kshs 0.53 trillion project, the foundation will put up and manage 517 Tajiriba Spaces across the country.

During the construction phase, the project has the potential to generate tens of thousands of direct and indirect income opportunities.

More importantly, it is estimated that the entire project when complete will make possible the generation of 8,272,000 (2,068,000 direct and 6,204,000 indirect) new private sector income opportunities in Kenya within a period of 10 years. The undertaking will also sustain a host of support industries, security services, food suppliers and vendors.

The implementation strategy for Tajiriba Spaces will ensure that wherever possible, labour, goods and services are sourced locally in order to create new income opportunities, and support the local business community and economy.

The project will benefit neighborhood industries and businesses which will secure construction contracts and supply huge quantities of material inputs and services.

Many people will benefit from the new job opportunities that will arise during the construction phase and later during the operational phase.

Interns will also get an opportunity to gain skills that will later boost their employability.

CHAPTER FOUR

CONCLUSION

Kenya has a huge infrastructure deficit. This dearth is especially evident in low-income urban and rural geographical locations.

The ramifications are that rural-urban migration is prevalent, out of 800,000 people joining the job market annually only 150,000 can get employment, and poverty is endemic.

Creation of income opportunities is the surest way to cushion households from the adverse effects of endemic poverty and preempt extreme and excessive concentration of wealth and economic power in existing cities and urban neighborhoods.

This write-up advocates for the establishment of public spaces in rural and remote neighborhoods throughout the country to deepen private sector penetration and to support entrepreneurship, inventions, discoveries, and to tap talent.

To bridge the infrastructure gap, overcome the opportunity shortage challenge and achieve the elusive double-digit economic growth annually, civil society, media and academia must be proactively engaged.

The intervention by nonprofits and public benefit organizations can reverse the state of affairs.

The write-up concludes that together the public, private and non-profit sectors can reduce unemployment from current rate of about 40 per cent to zero by 2030.

BIBLIOGRAPHY

Bayart, J-F. (1993). *The State in Africa: The Politics of the Belly*. New York: Longman.

CBK (2014). "Diaspora Remittances". Accessed on Sunday, February 01, 2015 from https://www.centralbank.go.ke/index.php/diaspora-remittances.

Chomsky Noam (1999). *Profit Over People: Neoliberalism and Global Order*. Seven Stories Press.

Cummings Ray (1973) [1922]. *Girl in the Golden Atom*. Hyperion Pr.

Duménil Gérard (2013). *The Crisis of Neoliberalism*. Harvard University Press.

Ekeh, P.P. (1975). "Colonialism and the Two Publics in Africa: A Theoretical Statement", *Comparative Studies in Society and History*, vol. 17, no 1.

Fukuyama Francis (1992). *The End of History and the Last Man*. New York: Free Press.

Gaines Anne (2001). *Tim Berners-Lee and the Development of the World Wide Web (Unlocking the Secrets of Science).* Mitchell Lane Pub Inc.

GoK (2007). Kenya Vision 2030: A Globally Competitive and Prosperous Kenya. Nairobi: Ministry of Planning and National Development and National Economic and Social Council (NESC).

Harvey David (2007) [2005]. *A Brief History of Neoliberalism.* Oxford University Press.

Huntington Samuel (1993). "The Clash of Civilizations". *Foreign Affairs.* Retrieved Sunday, February 01, 2015 from http://www.foreignaffairs.com/articles/48950/samuel-p-huntington/the-clash-of-civilizations.

Huntington Samuel (2011) [1996]. *The Clash of Civilizations and the Remaking of World Order.* Simon & Schuster.

Hyden, Goran (1980). *Beyond Ujamaa in Tanzania: Underdevelopment and an Uncaptured Peasantry.* London: Heinemann.

ILO (2014). *Global Employment Trends 2014: The Risk of a Jobless Recovery.* International Labour Organization.

Keynes, John Maynard (2011) [1936]. *The General Theory of Employment, Interest and Money*. CreateSpace Independent Publishing Platform.

Khamala Geoffreyson (2009) *Gender Dimension of Ethnic Conflicts in Kenya: The Case of Bukusu and Sabaot Communities*. MA Thesis, Kenyatta University, Kenya.

Khamala Geoffreyson (2014a). *The Perfect Theory: A Complete Unified Description of the Universe*. Tajiriba Foundation.

Khamala Geoffreyson (2014b). *What is Science! Science as an Adaptive Capacity*. Tajiriba Foundation.

Khamala Geoffreyson (2014c). *Is Science Religion*. Tajiriba Foundation.

Khamala Geoffreyson (2014d). *Wither Globalization Enter Connectedness*. Tajiriba Foundation.

Khamala Geoffreyson (2015a). *The Ultimate Theory: The Perfection Description of the Universe*. Tajiriba Foundation.

Khamala Geoffreyson (2015b). *Tajiriba Spaces: The Solution to Sub-Optimal Outcomes*. Tajiriba Foundation.

Kiernan Ben (1997). *The Pol Pot regime: Race, power and genocide in Cambodia under the Khmer Rouge, 1975–79.* New Haven, Conn: Yale University Press.

Leys Colin (1975). *Underdevelopment in Kenya, the Political Economy of Neo-Colonialism, 1964-1971.* London: Heinemann Educational Books.

Medema Steven G. (2007). "The Hesitant Hand: Mill, Sidgwick, and the Evolution of the Theory of Market Failure," *History of Political Economy,* 39(3), p p. 331-358.

Morgenthau Hans, Thompson Kenneth & Clinton David (2005) [1948]. *Politics Among Nations.* McGraw-Hill.

Muhammad Yunus (2009). *Creating a World Without Poverty: Social Business and the Future of Capitalism.* PublicAffairs.

Odinga Oginga (1968). *Not Yet Uhuru: The Autobiography of Oginga Odinga.* Nairobi; East African Educational Publishers Ltd.

Orbach, Barak (2013). "What Is Government Failure," *Yale Journal on Regulation Online,* 30, pp. 44-56.

Renato Cirillo (1978). *The Economics of Vilfredo Pareto.* Routledge.

UN (2014). World Population Prospects: The 2014 Revision. Geneva: United Nations.

UN HABITAT (2007). *State of the World's Cities 2010/2011.* Nairobi: United Nations Human Settlements Programme.

UNDP Human Development Report (2014). *Sustaining Human Progress: Reducing Vulnerabilities and Building Resilience.* New York: UNDP.

United Nations (2008). *World Urbanization Prospects: The 2007 Revision Population Database.* New York: UN.

United Nations (2014). *World Urbanization Prospects: The 2014 Revision.* New York: UN.

Wa Wamwere Koigi (2003). Negative Ethnicity: From Bias to Genocide.

World Bank (2005). World Development Indicators. Retrieved Thursday, January 29, 2015 from http://data.worldbank.org/country/kenya#cp_wdi.

World Bank (2014). "Kenya Overview". Retrieved on Thursday, January 29, 2015 from http://www.worldbank.org/en/country/kenya/overview.